MW00593719

Truth, Lies and Control

PRAISE FOR *TRUTH, LIES AND CONTROL*

Michael Letts, author of *Truth, Lies and Control*, has written an important book about today's trending political topics: life, liberty, property, and your right to self-defense. The new left is not what it seems, all roses and glitter. Letts takes a deeper look to the ugly hidden consequences of their policies and concludes the only way to fight their lies is with the truth.

-Chaplain Gordon Klingenschmitt, PhD
Pray In Jesus' Name, author of *How to Liberate the World in 30 Days*

While perusing the manuscript of *Truth, Lies and Control* by Michael Letts with Don Otis, I found it to be compelling reading with interesting anecdotes. It contains noteworthy statistics, and it intertwines society's ills with their parallels to be found in the days of the Bible. *Truth, Lies and Control* answers: Where did we go wrong in this nation and how do we get back on track?

-Jerry Newcombe, D.Min. Executive Director of Providence Forum, a division of Coral Ridge Ministries

A must-read for the Christian needing encouragement and a reminder they are on the winning side of the culture war. Letts and Otis take on the moral decay of American society through the lens of Truth and reason. By collecting and displaying salient examples and vetted research, the author(s) demonstrate the extent to which society has truly unraveled, but *Truth, Lies and Control* lives up to its title and helps the reader find hope in this upside-down world.

-Dorothy A. Logan, Author of *The Unraveling: The American Fabric Undone*

Truth
Lies *and*
Control

FINDING HOPE *in an*
Upside-Down World

MICHAEL A. LETTS
with DON S. OTIS

NASHVILLE

NEW YORK • LONDON • MELBOURNE • VANCOUVER

Truth, Lies *and* Control
Finding Hope in an Upside-Down World

© 2025 Michael A. Letts with Don S. Otis

All rights reserved. No portion of this book may be reproduced, stored in a retrieval system, or transmitted in any form or by any means—electronic, mechanical, photocopy, recording, scanning, or other—except for brief quotations in critical reviews or articles, without the prior written permission of the publisher.

Published in New York, New York, by Morgan James Publishing. Morgan James is a trademark of Morgan James, LLC. www.MorganJamesPublishing.com

All Scripture is taken from the New International Version (NIV) of the Bible. Copyright© 1973, 1978, 1984, 1985, 2011. Zondervan Bible Publishers, Grand Rapids, Michigan 49506

Proudly distributed by Publishers Group West®

Morgan James BOGO™

A **FREE** ebook edition is available for you or a friend with the purchase of this print book.

CLEARLY SIGN YOUR NAME ABOVE

Instructions to claim your free ebook edition:
1. Visit MorganJamesBOGO.com
2. Sign your name CLEARLY in the space above
3. Complete the form and submit a photo of this entire page
4. You or your friend can download the ebook to your preferred device

ISBN 9781636984506 paperback
ISBN 9781636984513 ebook
Library of Congress Control Number:
2024933500

Cover and Interior Design by:
Chris Treccani
www.3dogcreative.net

Morgan James is a proud partner of Habitat for Humanity Peninsula and Greater Williamsburg. Partners in building since 2006.

Get involved today! Visit: www.morgan-james-publishing.com/giving-back

ACKNOWLEDGMENTS

No one gets through life without help. When you go through tough times, and we all do, we need people in our corner who believe in us, who encourage us. My parents, Rev. Dennis R. Letts and Mary I. Letts have stood with me during good times and challenging times. Without their love and support, and most important, their time-tested values, this book would never have happened. To my wife, Karen S. Letts who has been a beacon of hope, a giver of life, and a steady companion. Her belief in our mission, our ideas, and our outreach have never wavered. To the thousands of police, First Responders, Veterans – those who risk their lives to keep us safe, we are all indebted to you for your service, your sacrifice, your perseverance. This is a time when our great nation has slid into collective madness. It has descended on us like a toxic cloud, poisoning the very institutions and values that make us great. Stay strong. I am your biggest fan, supporter, friend. You have lived the values and principles I write about in this book. To my fellow patriots, I salute you. To my late friend, Dr. Jerry Falwell of Liberty University. It was his non-compromising faith and values – in truth, in hope, in faith – that you will see in the pages of this book. It was my honor to serve as his assistant but even more my privilege to learn and grow in my own values serving alongside him. He was a great mentor and friend. There are others who have never wavered in their support for me or the vital message this book contains. It is rare to find this kind of loyalty. My marvelous staff at In-VestUSA. My senior advisor, Chip Dupre, a true and dedicated friend with principles that make a difference for America's future generations. In-VestUSA advisors, friends, and volunteers who truly have a heart for our First Responders and Veterans. To Kentuckyianna Jones, (Michael Barrick) who made Treasure Trove Park in Mammoth Cave Kentucky a successful family entertainment park dedicated to helping Veterans/First Responders. To America's True Heroes, Jimmy Oliver whose big heart for America's Heroes is on constant display. To Ben Bolding, a true In-VestUSA fellow officer who served with great distinction. To my political mentors with whom I had the honor of serving the warm people of South Carolina for 30 years on the Council of Governments. To US Senator Strom Thurmond along with other Senators and US Congress members too numerous to mention without fear of overlooking anyone. Governors from across America, especially South Carolina Governor Henry McMaster, a friend for many years. To the Council members, and state legislators nationwide, and most importantly national, state, county, city, and local law enforcement chiefs, officers, as well as the same with Fire Departments and EMS personnel. Without the guidance and friendship of national religious leaders who frequented Liberty University during my tenor, I would be remiss if I failed to acknowledge and thank the many friends in the entertainment industry including Erick Roberts, Billy Bob Thorton, Gary Sinise, Sir Earl Toon (Kool and the Gang), Dolly Parton, and Cleve and Scott, my producers with Imagination Bay Entertainment. To my friends and publicist, Jerry McGlothlin (Special Guests), and Don Otis (Veritas Communications) who enable you, the reader, to be a part of the values and principles we have embraced. Lastly, to Terry Whalin at Morgan James Publishing for believing in this book and to Kathi Macias whose expertise as an editor pulled it all together. We are united together to restore America to her glorious heritage. Let Freedom Ring!

CONTENTS

INTRODUCTION

How Did We Get Here?

We know something is wrong. You do. I do. Even people with little or no faith know. We can blame the mainstream media, anarchists, racists, socialists, or myriad other so-called causes. But we know what we feel; maybe it's intuition. And we know what we see; we aren't blind. There is no getting around it. We are watching the slow collapse of our country's values, which past generations fought and died for. They hoped to pass these along to you and me, to our children and grandchildren. Sadly, that may not be possible. Those values are eroding fast—faster than any of us ever could have imagined.

Nearly 2,700 years ago, a Jewish prophet named Isaiah prophesied to a decaying nation. The people had fallen into widespread corruption, and the once great nation was about to collapse. Ironically—or providentially—Isaiah's name means "Yahweh is salvation." God is salvation. The majority of the people didn't care. They sacrificed their babies, practiced homosexuality, and replaced monotheistic worship with countless alternative lifestyles and ideologies. In other words, despite the economic and political blessing they had, they forgot who they were. They forgot their unique place in the world. They gave up that place even though they knew they were exceptional. They were *chosen*.

Isaiah wrote, "Woe to those who call evil good and good evil, who put darkness for light and light for darkness …. Woe to those who are wise in their own eyes and clever in their own sight" (Isaiah 5:20-21). But it's more than calling evil good. It's calling what's right wrong, and vice-versa. It's creating confusion, eliminating moral truth, ignoring what's right in front of our eyes. Does it seem strange to see pro-abortion picketers with signs that read "abortion is health care" and "abortion saves lives"? Is it paradoxical, both morally and intellectually, that we have so-called healthcare providers who lop off the genitals of prepubescent boys or girls in the name of compassion? How about those girls who have trained hard to win swim meets or races only to find a man standing in their locker room, pretending to be one of them so he can compete against them—and no doubt win?

You know the issues, and you are likely as troubled about them as I am. Perhaps you feel helpless and hopeless. I urge you not to give up. Do not give in to the *zeitgeist*. Let me be clear. The prevalence of this sort of thinking is evil. Like the prophet Isaiah, we must speak up against evil regardless of what people want to hear or how they may react. We must protect the innocent. We must push back against wrong ideas that are infecting our great nation like cancer. I have spent time in the military, I am an ordained independent Southern Baptist minister, and I have worked hard to support those who are most under attack—our great men and women in uniform. It has been part of my calling, my mission, and my delight. Upfront, I want you to know that I am a man of faith. I am also a man who firmly believes faith without action is pointless.

In the following chapters you will learn some things you may not have known. You may find yourself angry and upset. You may weep over some of the stories you read. My goal is not to depress or discourage you—just the opposite. I want you to be aware and *act*. There is plenty you *can* do. The worst thing good people can do is to remain silent amid evil. Listen to what the great German martyr Dietrich Bonhoeffer wrote before he died at the hands of the Nazis: "The messengers of Jesus will be hated to the end of time. They will be blamed for all the divisions which rend cities and homes. Jesus and his disciples will be condemned on all sides for leading the nation astray; they will be called crazy fanatics and disturbers of the peace."[1]

There are many others who feel concerned about the state of our nation and world, as I do. I never thought I would be publishing a book about the issues we will be talking about in the following chapters. If you had told me twenty years ago that I would be talking about defunding the police, transgenderism, and woke education, I would not have believed you. But here we are. And talk we must. I have personally been frustrated and disappointed by the violence and crime, often from explosive anger we see in America today. Perhaps you feel the same. What I will strive to do in this book is to help you understand how we ended up in the place we are today—and what we can do about it.

What makes this book different from what others have already said and are saying? While the issues are mostly the same, what I want you to come away with is a firm understanding of how these moral and sociological issues are connected, which I firmly believe they are. And I believe the connections will become more apparent as we work our way through the first chapter.

CHAPTER ONE

Sowing Seeds of Destruction

"As behavior worsens, the community adjusts its standards so that conduct once thought reprehensible is no longer deemed so."
–Robert H. Bork

Officer Christopher Fitzgerald was new to the Temple University Police Force. His father had served as Police Chief in Ft. Worth, Texas, and Fitzgerald wanted to follow in his footsteps. He wanted to serve. At the age of thirty-one, with a wife and four children at home, he intervened in a car-jacking. The perpetrator, eighteen-year-old Miles Pfeffer, pulled a gun and shot Officer Fitzgerald in the head. He then rifled through the officer's pockets for anything of value. Then, as he stood over the officer, he fired three more shots into his face and torso before fleeing. In earlier Instagram posts, Pfeffer had written,

"Work smart not hard make stupid decisions face stupid consequences." Apparently, he failed to take his own advice.

Philadelphia Mayor Jim Kenney said he was "heartbroken and outraged" by the death and pledged, "The City will continue to work with Temple Police to support them during this difficult time." Nice words; that's what politicians have to do—say what's expected of them at the appropriate moment. In Kenney's city, robberies in which perpetrators used guns are up 60 percent, property crimes more than 30 percent, and commercial burglaries a staggering 50 percent. Overall violent crime is surging, and robberies have more than doubled.[2]

I can hear it now. "If we would only ban handguns, these crimes would not be so prevalent." How many times have we heard this? Yet, in 2020, the City Council in Philadelphia approved a $33 million decrease in police funding.[3] Is it possible that by defunding police departments nationwide we have opened Pandora's Box of consequences? Is it possible there is a correlation between defunding the police and emboldening the criminals? Let's look at another example.

In Austin, Texas, a liberal city that cut a third of its police budget (the largest cut of any major city in America), the city has seen a 71 percent increase in homicides.[4] In downtown Austin, street racers took over a large part of the city, drifting in the middle of the street, setting off fireworks, as bystanders looked on at the chaos. One law enforcement officer was injured, and several police cars were damaged. Council Member Alison Alter happened upon the street takeover and called 911. She was on hold for nearly half an hour. Ironically, it was Alter and one other council member who had recently voted against a one-year contract extension between the city and the Austin Police.

Still, even when confronted by the consequences of their own misplaced leadership, these defund-the-police proponents don't change. Instead, they double-down on their positions. One of the council members who also voted against the contract extension said, "Accountability is critical to maintain the bonds of trust between the police and the community [but] we need more police officers in this city, patrolling our streets, downtown, and major events. We need police responding to calls for service." Does this Orwellian doublespeak make any sense to you? When council members talk about accountability, are they speaking about the hoodlums who are taking over the streets, committing homicides, or breaking into businesses? Of course not. They only want law enforcement to be accountable, not criminals.

Austin and Philadelphia are not the only cities facing anarchy. It's happening in the suburbs too. Leleh Kashani owns a rental home in Lynnwood, Washington, a town in the next county north of Seattle. The home was taken over by squatters during the pandemic. Evictions were prohibited by the liberal state government, despite the fact that the owner and multiple nearby residents begged and pleaded with local law enforcement to do something. Finally, about thirty police officers, including a SWAT team, took part in a raid that cleared out the property. Police say fifty-two cars, some of them stolen, along with drugs and firearms, were found on the property. "They are a bunch of criminals" said Kashani. "They took over the house, and we couldn't collect a dollar of rent, and we have a mortgage."

After the property was cleared, the owner changed the locks, but the squatters came back and broke in anyway. "They should at least be arrested for breaking in," Kashini said. Sadly, that didn't happen. According to state and local authorities, ensuring the squatters don't return is the property owner's responsibility.[5] Is it any wonder people are leaving left-leaning states in droves? California has lost half a million people in the last year alone. In fact, migration out of blue states run by progressives puts greater pressure on red states where people relocate to seek lower taxes and greater freedom. Now imagine property owners fully armed in the State of Washington trying to protect their property from thieves, drug addicts, and looters. Is this what we want? A law without consequences is only advice. Do you know who knows this better than anyone? Criminals and anarchists.

These are only three stories, but they appeared in the news on a single day. They represent what is becoming the norm in the land of the free and the home of the brave. But these are only the tip of the iceberg. How in the world did we get to a place where criminals are treated with sympathy and compassion, while victims are acceptable collateral damage? Why are liberal city council members, governors, congressmen, or schoolboards so unable to connect the dots between their failed ideas and the carnage that follows? Let's begin with what ought to be obvious.

Why Worldviews Matter

Theologian and author Os Guinness wrote, "Most of the time our worldviews are unconscious, but even when we don't see them, we see *by* them." Worldviews matter because they determine how we act. If our worldviews are broken or faulty, we draw wrong conclusions even if we think they are correct. It's a bit scary. Guinness went on to say that we live in a world where we "derive our worldviews from a variety of sources—parents, education, cultural background, experiences, and discoveries . . . we think with our worldview, not *about* it."[6] In other words, we all have a worldview, even if it isn't clearly articulated.

Have you heard the statement, "Well, that may be true for you but it's not true for me"? Or, how about this one? "What consenting adults do is none of my business." Or, "You be you, and I'll be me." The common denominator in all of these is a worldview that says, "What I do is no one else's business. I know what's best for me." Sounds good, doesn't it? None of us likes to be told we are wrong, let alone how we should act. We believe everything about the choices we make is our business, and ours alone. We are the captain of our soul, and we demand it so. The Judeo-Christian tradition teaches differently. It teaches us to think of others before ourselves. To think about community. To consider how our choices will impact those around us. To respect our vows of marriage, as well as our neighbor's property or possessions.

For some of us, me included, our worldview is informed and formed by beliefs that transcend self. We believe moral truth can be known, that it matters, that it was given to us by our Creator. We are all part of something bigger than ourselves. Today, however, many believe they are bigger than the collective whole. God never designed us to live autonomously. He created us to live in community, in harmony, in peace and safety. How do I know this? Because He gave us rules to live by. He did it for our good, not just for His. Think about that for a moment. You may think the Ten Commandments are impediments to your freedom, but the truth is exactly the opposite. Those who adopt and live by a worldview that transcends their own ideas of right or wrong find moral truth as a light to guide them.

What's the big deal about people wanting to live autonomous lives? Why should we care? As the late social scientist Robert Bellah said, "We live through institutions." There are collective values to a healthy society, mores or norms that guide that society's behavior. These ideas don't come from nothingness; they come from our shared values. In the case of American values, they come from our Judeo-Christian heritage. As Bellah went on to say, "Democracy requires a degree of trust that we often take for granted." Our institutions, he said, are "patterned ways of living together." When we talk about liberal worldviews, they matter because they infringe upon the values and rights of others. "Philosophical liberals are those who believe that our problems can be solved by autonomous individuals, a market economy, and a procedural state."[7]

Now let's look at the ancient Hebrews again for a moment. There was a time in their history when they forgot the rules God gave them and decided to make news ones. ". . . another generation grew up, who knew neither the LORD nor what he had done for Israel" (Judges 2:10b) Let's stop there for a moment. The parents stopped teaching their children about God and how they ought to conduct their lives. This was their job then, even as it is our job today. Not schools. Not the media. Not scout leaders. Not even well-meaning youth pastors. It is a parental responsibility, period.

Because the Israelites forsook what they knew to be true, God became angry with them, and He gave them into the hands of their enemies. Judges 2:15 and 17 says, "They were in great distress . . . they would not listen . . . They quickly turned from the way of their ancestors, who had been obedient to the LORD's commands." This is a sad state of affairs for a once-great people. It is easy for us to look backward, to look at decisions made by people from the past and say, "How foolish could they be?" We don't think this is us; we're smarter than that. But are we? Finally, the Scriptures tells us that in those days "everyone did as he saw fit" (21:25). This is a sad end, an unnecessary end. But when we adopt false worldviews, worldviews that remove God and a moral authority from the picture, there are always negative outcomes.

Worldviews are the start of anything good or bad. They drive our behavior. They are like tiny dictators on our shoulder. If you are anything like me, you have been thinking about how quickly our culture and the rule of law are crumbling. This didn't happen overnight. It didn't happen with any single president or political party, though we've certainly seen it escalate under liberal leadership. Why? Because this is part of their worldview. For example, if you think guns should be banned, your worldview is that guns are bad and people are basically good (this is humanism). I believe differently. People are flawed. They sin. They make poor choices. As I look backward fifty years, the seeds of what has come to fruition in our country today are creating their toxic bloom in our culture. I will elaborate on each, but you will quickly see some of the connections to how we arrived at this moment in time.

No-Fault Divorce

No-Fault Divorce was first introduced into law in California in 1969. Social scientists have pointed to the lower rates of divorce since these laws were enacted. What they don't tell us is that the rates of cohabitation have exploded. When couples living together split, they never show up in divorce statistics. This is another example of so-called experts drawing the wrong conclusions. Again, we can ask, "What's the big deal? Why is marriage so important if people are living in a committed relationship?"

Let's tackle the first part of this question. In her seminal book, *Second Chances*, Judith Wallerstein says, "Divorce has ripple effects that touch not just the family involved, but our entire society." She goes on to suggest each divorce is the death of a small civilization.[8] The myth of a "good divorce" is the byproduct of a culture unwilling to examine the actual fallout. "Indeed, it is the children of divorce who taught us very early that to be separated from their father was intolerable," says Wallerstein. ". . . fathers remain a significant psychological presence in the lives of children after divorce. The father is part of the child's emotional life, a factor in the child's self-esteem, self-image, aspirations, and relationships with the opposite sex."[9] This well-established research refutes the idea of so-called toxic masculinity. To be sure, some men are abusive deadbeats who abandon their families, but this is the exception rather than the norm. Most men are good husbands and fathers. Most are responsible. Most want to be involved in their children's lives. To denigrate men is to put society in peril.

When we use the term "no-fault" to describe a divorce, we do so to keep from stigmatizing the death of the relationship. But the truth is more complicated. Divorce happens for many reasons—often a cheating spouse, abuse, abandonment, addictions, etc. I am not trying to guilt anyone because they have been through a divorce. That is not my purpose here. Rather, what I am saying is that divorce has an impact on society. It weakens us on a collective level. As much as we would like to tell ourselves how resilient kids of divorce are, the truth is they struggle more academically, in relationships, with substance abuse, and have higher rates of incarceration. This doesn't sound like resilience to me. It sounds more like a cry for help.

No-fault divorce, easy divorce, cohabitation—these all create a weaker society, one where the traditional commitments deteriorate and permission is given, psychologically and legally, to "do what seems right in our own eyes." When we allow damage to our "little societies," it becomes easier to damage our big society. It becomes more expendable. Unnecessary. Antiquated. In the words of Charles Colson, "Without commitment to community, individual responsibility quickly erodes."

Roe v. Wade

Roe v. Wade was a landmark decision by the Supreme Court that ruled the Constitution allowed room for abortion. This was 1973, and since that time, 63 million babies have been exterminated. Let's put this number in perspective. If the U.S. experienced a nuclear strike that wiped out nearly 20 percent of our population, that would be the equivalent number of unborn children killed. Nearly half of all women will choose to abort a child at some point in their lifetime. Abortion is the most common medical procedure in the country. In America, the topic of abortion is discussed; actual abortions are not. The devastating long-term effects are kept secret.

Therapist and author Teri Reisser says, "Pro-choice activists frequently claim that 'religious dogma' and outmoded sexual taboos are the primary source of personal and cultural resistance to abortion. But when a woman has just learned she is pregnant, deeper instincts—which transcend both her moral code and her circumstances—quickly begin to stir. The knowledge that a new human being is growing inside of her sets off an unmistakable inner spark. Whether she acknowledges it or not, her universe is a different place from that point on."[10] Reisser doesn't equivocate when it comes to abortion. Most post-abortion women carry an "abortion wound" but never specifically identify it or understand its ongoing impact on their lives.

Sadly, the majority of Americans have come to value personal choice above moral truth. This is certainly true in abortion. Our personal rights, our feelings, our happiness—they take precedence over all else. This has not always been the case. Personal sacrifice, responsibility, the value of human life has been part of our Judeo-Christian heritage. We have taken "Life, Liberty, and the Pursuit of Happiness" found in the Constitution and removed the word "Life" when it comes to abortion. But why have I included this as part of this chapter?

I firmly believe every life has value. If God created us in His image and likeness, we honor Him by honoring one another, by honoring life. When the Supreme Court ruled on Roe, it ruled that unborn human life could be sacrificed for convenience.

The ruling devalued *all* human life, making it less consequential at the expense of another human being. When we devalue the most vulnerable in a society, we weaken that society's moral constitution by elevating expediency under the mantra of choice.

School Prayer

In 1962, the Supreme Court ruled prayer in public schools unconstitutional. In the 18th, 19th, and most of the 20th centuries, prayer was part of public education, as was Bible reading. Why is this such a big deal? The effect of the 1962 ruling was to remove the practice of acknowledging God from the minds of impressionable youth. Today, some teachers and schoolboards want free access to our children so they can indoctrinate them in humanist philosophies, woke ideologies, and values that are contrary to what many parents believe or want taught to their offspring. And isn't this exactly what's been happening? Some teachers and schoolboard members are convinced they know what's best for our children—and are working very hard to indoctrinate them accordingly.

Debbie Squires is on the Michigan Education Committee. When the topic of school choice came before the board, Squires clearly articulated how she felt about parental involvement in education. "[Educators] are the people who know best about how to serve children, that's not necessarily true of an individual resident," Squires said. "I'm not saying they don't want the best for their children, but they may not know what actually is best from an education standpoint."[11] Squires and countless educators, schoolboard members, and administrators want free reign over our kids and grandkids. Standing in their way are parents. Standing in their way are religious and moral values that put parents in charge. And yet parents are the ones who know best how to educate their children.

The Age of Aquarius

The Age of Aquarius became synonymous with the hippie and New Age movements of the '70s. The rise of scientific rationalism, combined with the fall of religious influence, became a dominant theme—alternative ideas, rejection of the old and acceptance of the new. The old was bad, the new was good. Experimenting and experiences became a rite of passage. Traditional beliefs and religion were the "opiate of the masses," keeping people in bondage. I mention this because it was a powerful influence on a generation that rejected right and wrong, truth and error, faith, and traditional disbelief. The widespread experimentation with drugs, sex, and rebellion against "the man" set the stage for where we find ourselves today.

The spirit of Aquarius is still alive and well. It animates education, politics, and even woke business. Is it any wonder that Woodstock—allegedly all about love and peace—was called "An Aquarian Exposition"?

Vietnam Protests

During that same time period, Vietnam protests—predominantly by leftist intellectuals—began on college campuses. The Students for a Democratic Society (SDS) played a prominent role in opposing U.S. involvement in the war. A growing number of mostly young people, who rejected authority and embraced the counterculture, rejected America's involvement in Vietnam. Even Martin Luther King called the war "a blasphemy against all that America stands for." But what did America stand for? At the time, more than fifty years ago, America was struggling with its identity. If supporting South Vietnam from being overrun by Communist North Vietnam wasn't worth fighting for, what was?

What's the connection between Vietnam protests and where we find ourselves today? It comes down to a single word: rebellion. It was a rebellion against American values, equated to combating fascism and communism. Universities became infected with liberal elitists who stirred hate against the system, which they saw as more corrupt than what was happening in the gulags. If we call them idealists, that implies they had ideals. Instead, what they started back then was a dismantling of trust in our great nation. As flawed as we have been at times in our history, we remain a beacon of light and hope to the rest of the world. If you doubt this, all you need to do is look at our southern border to see how many people want in.

What were we fighting for in Vietnam? Freedom. America has always wanted other people to experience the freedom we have enjoyed. We believe—and rightly so—that freedom enables people and nations to thrive and survive. It lifts us out of poverty, gives us hope, incentive, and a better future.

Stonewall Inn

Stonewall Inn was a gay club in New York. At a time when it was illegal to solicit same-sex relationships, the club was open to drag queens, homosexuals, and even kids from the streets. In 1969, police raided the Mafia-run gay bar—legally and with a warrant—and found bootlegged alcohol. They used this as a pretext for a crackdown and arrested patrons who soon started pushing back and rioting. Gay people were used to running from the police, but this time they were the ones on the advance, while the men in uniform were on the retreat.

Stonewall is synonymous with gay rights—or should I now say, special rights. What began that night in 1969 is now a driving force to change our society. No longer do gays and lesbians simply want the right to engage in sexual activity, once deemed a mental disorder by the psychological community; they want full and complete acceptance by everyone (more on this later). Distress over one's sexual orientation remained in the Diagnostic and Statistical Manual of Mental Disorders until 2013, with homosexuality considered "pathological sexuality." Not surprisingly, gay activists celebrated the removal of homosexuality from the American Psychological Society's list of mental disorders. "This represents the culmination of a decade-long battle," declared Ronald Gold of the National Gay Task Force. "We've won."

What does homosexuality and its growing number of permutations have to do with how we got to where we are today? It opened the door for any and all sexual activities as acceptable, normal, and without judgment. Nothing can be forbidden because nothing can be judged as aberrant. What's considered normal? Anything that any person *feels* is normal. There are no longer any boundaries. We will soon see pederasty (sex between adult men and boys) become normalized unless we put a stop to this nonsense and see it for what it is: an evil that inflicts great harm on children at the expense of personal desire.

It was Ronald Reagan who famously said, "Freedom is never more than one generation away from extinction." We don't pass it to our children in the bloodstream. It must be fought for, protected, and handed on for them to do the same. If we don't, one day we will spend our sunset years telling our children and our children's children what it was once like in the United States where men were free. Reagan had lived through the turbulent era of the '60s and '70s and knew what lay ahead for us if we didn't recognize and begin to appreciate our blessings. Listed below are the years when each of these movements started.

- Removal of prayer from public schools, 1962
- Hippie movement, 1967
- Vietnam protests, 1967
- Woodstock counterculture festival, 1969
- Stonewall riots, 1969
- Legalization of abortion, 1973

Look at these dates. What do you notice? They all started within about a ten-year span, and they all changed our culture as we know it. We are one generation away from those dates today. From pushing radical rebellion, the legal killing of the unborn, dismissing God from schools, welcoming LGBTQ lifestyles as an alternative to traditional families, and the weakening of marriages, we have begun reaping what we've sown. Each of these issues points full-circle to what we're seeing play out in our culture today.

CHAPTER TWO

It's not about Guns: Why the Second Amendment Matters

"Laws that forbid the carrying of arms. . . disarm only those who are neither inclined nor determined to commit crimes. . . Such laws make things worse for the assaulted and better for the assailants; they serve rather to encourage than to prevent homicides, for an unarmed man may be attacked with greater confidence than an armed man."[12]

–Thomas Jefferson

Deshawn Thomas was seen on video standing on a street corner in downtown St. Louis in broad daylight. Next to him was a homeless man seated on a curb. The twenty-three-year-old Thomas methodically loaded a pistol, pointed it at the back of the homeless man's head, and pulled the trigger—execution style. An eyewitness is heard saying, "Oh, my God, he just f---ing killed him!"

The George Soros-backed St. Louis Circuit Attorney, Kim Gardner, was already under scrutiny for her handling of the prosecution of twenty-one-year-old Daniel Riley. Daniel was out on bail after violating his bond multiple times. While driving, he struck teenager Janae Edmondson, who was visiting St. Louis with her family for a volleyball tournament. Riley was speeding, failed to yield, and caused a collision, ultimately striking and pinning Edmondson, who had both her legs amputated after sustaining injuries from the crash. When pressed by a reporter about the incident, Gardner said, "But what we can control is we're going to fight very hard for justice in spite of the vitriol, the hate, the racist attacks." Perhaps you are asking yourself the same question I am: "What in the world does race have to do with anything?"[13]

I can give hundreds of examples like these. Hoodlums out on bond, committing more crimes, and weak or non-existent enforcement by liberal judges, prosecutors, or communities. When I say it's not about guns, here's what I mean. Criminals will always find ways to hurt others; that's why they need to be locked up. We do no one any favors by showing compassion to people who see our compassion as weakness and then turn around and take advantage of the system. Let me take a moment to explain the problem with this kind of compassion. Actually, compassion is the wrong word because compassion is what we show when someone deserves a second chance, and few career criminals do. Let's examine the dilemma too often ignored and rarely understood about the so-called compassionate approach to criminals.

The Problem with Mercy

For just a moment, suppose Deshawn Thomas came before the judge after shooting the homeless man and begged for mercy. "Your honor, I don't know what came over me. I ask the court to show mercy. I promise to be a model citizen from now on." What happens when a parent or a judge shows mercy? *It weakens the law.* If every parent shows mercy—and some do—to a misbehaving child, the parental authority ceases to be taken seriously. A judge who shows mercy more times than he upholds the rule of law weakens the very law he is sworn to uphold. But there is another problem with mercy.

If a child punches her brother, the parent has a decision to make. If she shows mercy, the child who was punched in the face doesn't receive justice—and justice is what backs the law. Too much mercy enables, rather than prevents, further bad behavior. If you are a Christian reading this, you know this is the same dilemma God has. He delights to show mercy. He wants to show mercy. Showing mercy is His nature and character. But as I said earlier, laws without consequences are merely advice. Justice and punishment for wrongdoing uphold and reinforce the law. How did God show mercy for our sin and still sustain His moral law? By sending His Son, Jesus, to take our penalty for wrongdoing. I realize we can't do this in our society, but the need to show mercy and justice is clear.

Here is another aspect to mercy. It is always easier for us to show mercy when the perpetrator is remorseful or repentant. As I have discovered countless times while working with the police, a person's attitude is key to how they are treated by law enforcement. When we watch criminals run from the police, disrespect law enforcement, flip them off, or scream about their rights, it doesn't improve their chances of receiving mercy, and rightly so. Here is the real kicker in all this. More than 70 percent of all criminal suspects released from jail without bail go on to be rearrested for committing more crimes.[14]

The California Judicial Council recently required counties to enforce an "emergency bail schedule." Enforce is the wrong word because what really happened with this requirement is that counties were forced to release thousands of criminals. Bail for certain crimes was dramatically reduced, many to zero dollars. The recidivism rates (the rate at which people commit new crimes) skyrocketed. This is precisely what happens when we show too much mercy. When liberal policies allow criminals out of their punishment, it puts all law-abiding citizens at risk. It forces them to consider what they need to do to protect themselves. Thomas Jefferson clearly understood this principle. The Second Amendment exists to protect law-abiding citizens from the lawless *and* from an out-of-control government.

It's not about the Guns

If you have been to Israel, you know that men and women across this tiny nation carry semiautomatic guns, particularly when they are often hitchhiking from one assignment to the next. If you remember back to 1973, Israel fought the Yom Kippur War or what was called the Ramadan War by their Muslim neighbors. A coalition of Arab states launched a surprise attack on the Jewish state on Yom Kippur, the Day of Atonement, the Jews' high holy day. Israel had to mobilize quickly to repel the invaders and to defend three separate fronts. Self-defense is not only a personal right to Israelis; it has become a life-and-death necessity—clearly illustrated in the latest terrorist attack by Hamas on Israel in October 2023.

When I say it is not about guns, I mean it is not the law-abiding citizens we need to worry about; it's criminals. Why is this distinction so hard for some people to recognize? We need to ask ourselves this important question: Who exactly are the people using guns to commit crimes? If we are serious about getting answers to this question, perhaps we can pinpoint the population of people most responsible. Let's look at the facts.

Violent crime is down and has been declining for decades; this is clearly not what the media want you to know. Rather, they are bent on pushing an agenda that removes your Second Amendment rights. A Heritage Foundation study offers some astonishing results.

1. Violent crime is down and has been on the decline for decades.
2. The principal public safety concerns with respect to guns are suicides and illegally owned handguns, not mass shootings.
3. A small number of factors significantly increase the likelihood that a person will be a victim of a gun-related homicide.
4. Gun-related murders are carried out by a predictable pool of people.
5. Higher rates of gun ownership are not associated with higher rates of violent crime.
6. There is no clear relationship between strict gun-control legislation and homicide or violent crime rates.

7. Legally owned firearms are used for lawful purposes much more often than they are used to commit crimes or suicide.

8. Concealed carry permit holders are not the problem, but they may be part of the solution.[15]

Think about this: 80 percent of gun-related crimes are committed by people with illegally own firearms. Recidivist violent offenders are responsible for the majority of gun violence. Passing strict gun-control laws will not make us safer; it will make us more vulnerable. And did you know more people are stabbed to death every year than are killed with rifles? This little-known fact is never mentioned by gun-control advocates. Here is another unmentioned fact: half of all gun deaths in this country are suicide, not homicides. When liberal district attorneys or judges release criminals into the public, those very district attorneys and judges—not the guns themselves and not law-abiding citizens—should be held responsible for putting all of us at risk.

What about AR-15s and other semiautomatic rifles? Does anyone need such high-capacity weapons? Does the Second Amendment really prevent gun owners from wielding such weapons? We have all heard the arguments. Nevertheless, law-abiding citizens commonly use these weapons in self-defense because they are versatile and easy to control. According to the Heritage Report, there are numerous instances where AR-15s have been used to *save* lives.

If gun-control laws work, it should be safe to assume that countries that pass the most restrictive gun-control laws have the lowest number of gun-related crimes, right? Isn't this what we have been force-fed by the left? Isn't this just common sense? No, it is not. When Australia passed the National Firearms Act, gun violence should have plummeted—but did it? Absolutely not. In fact, it had little effect on suicide and homicide rates. When Great Britain passed stringent gun-control legislation, citizens should have become safer, right? Wrong. Homicide and firearm deaths spiked.

What exactly does this data tell us? For one, we cannot fix the problem with gun-related deaths by giving away our Second-Amendment rights. Here is what the Amendment says: *A well-regulated Militia, being necessary to the security of a free State, the right of the people to keep and bear Arms, shall not be infringed.*

The security of a free state means we are enjoined by the U.S. Constitution to protect that free state. But protect it from what, exactly? From any and all people or groups that seek its destruction. We the people are encouraged to bear arms. When any entity tries to eliminate this right, they become an enemy of the state. We must see it this way, or we will give more ground to those who seek to reverse two centuries of freedoms enjoyed by American citizens.

The second thing this data tells us is that we keep talking about all the wrong things when it comes to gun control. It is not about guns; it is about the people who use them. No amount of legislation will change the truth that suicidal people who want to kill themselves or criminals who want to hurt others will be deterred. It simply does not work. And it is plain and obvious to anyone who is serious about the data. The obvious question then is, what is the blame for gun violence? Here is where it gets a bit more complicated, but let me mention a few factors that I believe contribute to gun violence. This is not meant to be an exhaustive list; it is meant to help us gain a better understanding of the contributing factors.

Why Gun Violence?

What does a progressive approach to gun control look like? These ideas are taken directly from their publicly stated solutions—and that's not all. The gun-control progressives also want to punish gun manufacturers for shooting deaths. That is about as absurd as punishing a boat manufacturer because a drunk operator crashed into someone's dock. Following are a few of the progressive's talking points—and wish list.

1. Ban the manufacture and sale of assault weapons and high-capacity magazines.
2. Regulate possession of existing assault weapons under the National Firearms Act.
3. Buy back the assault weapons and high-capacity magazines already in our communities.
4. Reduce stockpiling of weapons.[16]

We have already demonstrated that bans don't work. Neither does buying back weapons. This is a worthless waste of time and resources. Progressives say they want to keep guns out of dangerous hands, and then they push for no bail or reduced bail so criminals are free to commit new crimes. Does this make any sense to you? So where does the blame actually belong? Squarely on the perpetrators of these crimes—not on gun manufacturers.

Social science uses the term "multivariate analysis" to describe various classes or variables that impact an outcome. Let's look at some of the direct or indirect causes of violence.

Broken Families

No one really wants to talk about this as a cause of criminal behavior, but the statistics bear it out. In his book *Life without Father*, David Popenoe wrote, "Father absence is a major force lying behind many of the attention-grabbing issues that dominate the news: crime and delinquency; premature sexuality, and out of wedlock teen births; deteriorating educational achievement, depression, substance abuse."[17] Out-of-wedlock births have soared since 1970 (no surprise). A whopping 72 percent of African-American babies are now born out of wedlock. Forty percent of all births are now non-marital childbearing. This is clearly an unspoken epidemic. Boys who grow up without fathers are at high risk of gun violence.[18]

A culture that deifies individuality at the cost of losing their children is not a healthy society. We have sacrificed our children for our own self-interests. Popenoe comes right out and tells it like it is: "If we continue down the path of fatherlessness, we are headed for a social disaster."[19] While we are busy pointing at the guns, we have forgotten the most important duty of all—to our children.

Culture of Violence

Americans love their violence. It is part of Hollywood, part of gaming, part of the music industry. Yet when someone acts out violently in real life, we cringe and say, "How could that happen?" We watch kids acting out, emulating, copying, patterning, and then ask questions that have obvious answers. The left refers to violence as the oxygen of authoritarianism. That is nonsense, unless you redefine violence to fit your paradigm. These statements about violence do not mean all gamers or people who watch slasher movies are going to commit heinous crimes. However, those who regularly participate in such activities will most likely find themselves desensitized to violence. It is in this process that what once seemed reprehensible becomes normalized. Once a behavior is normalized, the next step becomes acceptance. In time, the things you once saw as wrong are now considered mainstream.

Any form of aberrant behavior—if I can use this term in today's world—is progressive. I don't mean this in a political way but in a psychological way. The more we engage in borderline behavior, the easier it becomes. Social-learning theory suggests a link between violent acting out and media depictions. Does watching violence and brutality on television increase aggression? This hypothesis is supported by the common-sense reasoning that daily exposure of dramatized violence hardens the watcher to brutality and may add specific items to his repertory of aggressive acts, as well as by modeling and imitating.[20]

The left places the blame for violence on authoritarian systems. Here is how they see it. "Gun violence cannot be abstracted from a broader culture of violence and authoritarianism that calls for more gun ownership, more police, and more national security. Moreover, both the gun industry and right-wing politicians who benefit from its profits are well-aware fear and extremism sell more guns and generate lucrative markets for the merchants of death. The right-wing response to school shootings is as disingenuous as it is morally corrupt."[21]

I personally find it repugnant to be lectured by people about gun violence when they are the same ones who encourage women to "shout their abortion." Again, the link between the left's depiction of violence always misses the key factors, not the least of which is the devaluation of human life.

Mental Disorders

When a shooter attacks children, it is hard not to believe the shooter has a mental disorder. When twenty-year-old Adam Lanza killed twenty-six people and himself at Sandy Hook Elementary School in Connecticut, he did so after first killing his mother. He then took four of his mom's guns and drove to the school, where he killed twenty first-grade children, ages six and seven, along with six adults, including four teachers, the principal, and the school psychologist. Why choose young innocent children? One theory is that he felt his own childhood had been ruined, so he wanted to "protect" these children from the pain he felt. What a twisted way to rationalize mass murder! As is the case with almost every shooting of this kind, the shooter took his own life after extinguishing the lives of the innocent.

In Santa Fe, Texas, in 2018, another deranged shooter killed ten and wounded another thirteen. Seventeen-year-old Dimitrios Pagourtzis started shooting in the school art room, then proceeded through the art hallway. Responding police officers then engaged Pagourtzis in a gunfight, which lasted for twenty-five minutes, before he was wounded and taken into custody. He was soon declared not mentally fit for trial. Pagourtzis wore a "born to kill" shirt when he was apprehended. Though he was a loner, there had been no major red flags. He too had planned to kill himself after the rampage.[22]

We can't blame mental illness for pulling the trigger. I believe wholeheartedly in personal responsibility and respect for others, but we are seeing more depression in youth than at any time in the past. Why is this? With endless news of hopelessness about the future, is it any wonder many feel they have no future? Is there nothing good to celebrate in the world? We can sow seeds of hope into the lives of young people. We can begin pointing out the good in the world, the good in children's lives. Mental illness can be a byproduct of hurt, rejection, abandonment, or anxiety. There is no better place to offset these toxic ingredients than the family. Yet as we have seen, the family has been in a state of decline for fifty years. And when I say family, I am not talking about alternative families; I am talking about nuclear families that instill positive values and provide reasonable limits.

Demonic Activity

Seriously—demonic activity? Yes, seriously. I know we live in the 21st century, so demon possession is only for the superstitious, right? The West has been influenced by the rationalism of the Enlightenment; we figure things out. We are far too sophisticated to believe in devils. But if you have doubts, take a moment to look up photos of Adam Lanza, Charles Manson, or Richard Ramirez ("The Night Stalker"). Psychiatrist and author M. Scott Peck was not a man of faith until he started counseling people he labeled evil. It was, in fact, seeing the evil that brought him to faith in Christ. "After many years of vague iden-tification with Buddhist and Islamic mysticism, I ultimately made a firm Christian commitment." What exactly was it that Peck saw? It was his encounters with people whose behaviors he could not explain as simple mental disorders. "There is, I suspect, something basically incomprehensible about evil. But if not incomprehensible, it is characteristically inscrutable. The evil always hide their motives with lies."[23]

Jesus called the devil "the father of lies." This is not by acci-dent because that's how evil operates. John 10:10 quotes Jesus as saying that the devil's intent is always to rob, kill, and destroy. To discount the presence of evil when someone guns down innocent children is to dismiss the possibility of the demonic. As Peck defines it, "Evil . . . is that force residing either inside or outside of human beings, that seeks to kill life or liveliness. And goodness is its opposite. Goodness is that which promotes life and liveliness."[24] Evil is in opposition to life.

Medical science fails in its ability to predict evil. Social sci-entists cannot predict evil, nor can counselors. It is, in the final analysis, an opening up of one's life and mind to the dark side, and its hold is progressive. Demonic influence can start with deep woundedness, rejection, trauma, bad decisions, or a lethal mix of each. It starts with a series of choices, generally getting progressively worse or increasingly dark (evil). It was C.S. Lewis who wrote, "The proper question is whether I believe in devils. I do. That is to say . . . some of these by the abuse of their free will, have become enemies to God."[25]

There is far too much evidence of demonic actors and activ-ities throughout history to justify unbelief of demonic influence or evil. We cannot intellectually ignore the possibility that some gun violence is the result of demonic influence. Whether we believe in God or his adversary, Satan, it is too much of a stretch to explain away some gun violence simply as mental disorders.

Where does this leave us? With many questions and few solid answers. What I do know for certain is that regardless of the source or origin of gun violence, the violence is never about the guns themselves. It is about fallen humanity. It is about evil. It is about hate or hurt. What we must not do is destroy our great Constitution and the Second Amendment because a few people draw the wrong conclusions. It is not just our right to bear arms; it is our duty as American citizens to protect our families, our community, and our nation. To do otherwise is to fall to the cowardly avarice for power that some people want for themselves. We need not apologize for owning guns or for using them legally. We need not cower in the face of opposition when the people who bark the loudest are setting prisoners free to commit new gun violence.

You will notice a recurring theme throughout this book. It is simply this: in the progressive's playbook, logic and common sense need not apply. People who think this way believe science is only for certain situations, not others. More importantly, they deny moral values that have been in place for centuries, for millennia even—and they work. As we will examine in the next chapter, common sense is out the window in the area that impacts education, business, public libraries, the arts, entertainment, and even sports.

CHAPTER THREE

Sex, Lies, and Confusion

"Homosexuality is a misguided search for love and affirmation
in sexual behavior that is contrary to nature."
—Stephen Black, ex-gay

Whe it comes to areas of modern culture dominated by lies, it is doubtful any could surpass the area of sexuality. This is the proverbial elephant in the room, sociologically and morally. To use another metaphor, it is the smoking gun, and it is impacting culture at an exponential pace. We are force-fed the necessity to accept all forms of sexual expression as if they are normal, though we know many are not. We feel the pressure from businesses, schools, legislation, advertising, and government mandate. This pressure is upfront and in our face. If we dare to question it, we are "haters," "bigots," or "prudes." If we object to drag shows in schools or recruiting kids for gay indoctrination, we are "homophobes." When we do speak up, our words may be labeled as "hate speech." We may lose our job. We may be accused of putting vulnerable people at risk. You get the picture. You've seen it. Perhaps you've experienced it.

One Arizona schoolboard member said the district should reject hiring teachers with Christian values because they are "not safe." School board member Tamillia Valenzuela wears cat ears and calls herself "a bilingual, disabled, neurodivergent Queer Black Latina." She made a motion to dissolve the partnership with a Christian University that provided student teachers to the Phoenix-Glendale school district. "Part of their [Christians'] values," said Valenzuela, "is to transform the culture with truth by promoting the Biblically informed values that are foundational to Western Civilization, including the centrality of the family, traditional sexual morality, and lifelong marriage between one man and one woman." Does this make any sense to you? A woman who dresses up as a cat has the audacity to lecture the rest of us about the dangers of "biblically informed values." On March 3, 2023, another Arizona school-board member, Hannah Grossman, said on Fox News that the district should reject hiring teachers with Christian values.[26]

What do Valenzuela and Grossman and others worry about? Our values—yours and mine. Traditional values. Judeo-Christian values. What do they want to replace them with? Their own values. No dissent. No debate. No serious look at themselves and how they might be harming culture. But who is to say Christian values about sexuality are any better than secular values? Who are we to say what is best? Those are reasonable questions. Let's take a look at the facts.

In her book *Adam and Eve After the Pill*, author Mary Eberstadt, a senior fellow at the Faith & Reason Institute in Washington, D.C., made some astounding conclusions about sexuality. "I'm using perfectly secular sources. There's no theology in this book," Eberstadt said. She looked at the long-term effects of the '60s and '70s sexual revolution that was supposed to liberate society from religiously uptight beliefs about marriage and romance. "I am saying this one thing, the sexual revolution, is the single least acknowledged causation of our social disarray." She suggests there is a secular religion that is competing for Christianity's moral foundations, seeking to redefine the family and undo any type of authoritarian structure.

"The traditional family and Christianity have always had enemies . . . That's what Marxism had in its sights. It wanted to destroy the family. And other utopians have always wanted to destroy the family." It is not by accident today that we see a face-off between schoolboards, teachers' unions, and parents trying to protect their kids. Most sane adults think the idea of teaching first-graders about sex is not just wrongheaded, it is evil. But desensitization is the goal. That is why parents must be vigilant and speak up. That's why we need to run for library boards, schoolboards, city councils, and county offices. Show up at meetings, ask questions, be diligent.

Eberstadt says the conventional wisdom was that reliable contraception would empower women by giving them opportunity to do their "family planning." The pill was seen as a panacea of sorts, a way to liberate women from unwanted pregnancies and give them freedom to have sex with whomever they wished whenever they wanted. Her research shows that with the introduction of artificial contraception, abortion and out-of-wedlock births all increased. On March 1, 2023, author Lauren Green confirmed Eberstadt's assertion when she said on FoxNews.com, "The skyrocketing of non-marital births and the breakup of families is on a scale never seen before, and it all starts with the 1960s."

Sexual Freedom and Real Life

The benefit of hindsight is we can look back and learn something about how to proceed today. The assumption is that we learn from our mistakes and adjust our worldviews. We adapt to consequences that teach us what is best or worst. The sexual revolution produced many outcomes that we can now look upon with clarity. Sadly, what many thought was liberation has turned out to be bondage.

The idea of recreational sex or "hooking up" is now commonplace, especially on campuses. There is no stigmatization about casual sex, sex without the emotional baggage, getting pregnant, or living with an STD (Sexually Transmitted Disease). "Everyone does it," as the old saying goes. "We're just having fun. After all, you only live once." Sadly, we live in a throwaway world where feelings are more important than commitment, and happiness trumps fidelity. What is the cost of this secular worldview?

- Sexually Transmitted Diseases and HIV—STDs such as herpes, chlamydia, gonorrhea, and syphilis are easily transmitted during oral, vaginal, or anal sex.
- Teen pregnancy—750,000 new cases each year. Teen parents are more likely to drop out of school, continue

to have nonmarital pregnancies, change jobs more frequently, be on welfare, and have mental and physical health problems.

- Emotional—Early sexual activity and multiple partners are associated with pain and suffering from broken relationships, a sense of betrayal and abandonment, confusion about romantic feelings, altered self-esteem, depression, and impaired ability to form healthy long-term relationships.[27]
- Deregulation of pornography—Consumers of pornography are three times more likely to pay prostitutes for sex and more than three times more likely to cheat on their spouse. The use of pornography has been growing every decade since the '60s. Repeated or obsessive viewing of pornography is associated in some men with a listlessness, boredom, a deadening of moral sensibilities, and even impotence when confronted with a real woman. As a result, people who use pornography rarely stay satisfied with its milder varieties. They demand ever more extreme displays to get the desired high from pornography. The result—paradoxical from the standpoint of sexual liberation—is "an addiction, tolerance and an eventual decrease in pleasure."[28]

These are just the tip of the iceberg. Compared with heterosexuals, the gay community experiences higher rates of STDs, substance abuse, domestic violence, depression, and suicide. The gay community doesn't want us to know these truths. If we dare to bring them out in the open, they say it is because gays and lesbians are persecuted and not accepted. This straw-man argument never changes the reality that a homosexual lifestyle leads to early death and disease. The life expectancy for a gay man in the U.S. is sixty, nearly twenty years less than a heterosexual male.[29]

If we treated homosexuality as the unhealthy lifestyle that it is, we would save many young lives. Instead, a licentious society encourages homosexuality and even celebrates it for an entire month every year, during which the community has its own parades, flags, and special celebrities. We put warning labels on cigarettes because they are lethal. Smoking and the use of illicit drugs like Fentanyl, or even obesity take lives prematurely. We want our young people to know that engaging in these activities is harmful to them, and rightly so. A homosexual lifestyle does the same, so why the silence? Imagine if Fentanyl addicts had an entire month each year to parade up and down city streets taking a hit, flying a Fentanyl flag, and seeing their cause—the right to engage in their drug addiction—normalized. Imagine if they did everything within their collective power to get the rest of us to think their drug addiction was a positive alternative lifestyle. Then imagine they tried to force you and me to accept what they were doing as something to celebrate. Finally, how would you feel if these addicts and their proponents pushed drug use in your child's school, suggesting to them they should try it?

As parents, we know we must sometimes tell our children things they do not want to hear or accept. That is what loving parents do. Why don't we do this as a society? Why can't we stand up and say, "I care about you, but you are harming yourself. There is a better and healthier way to live." Granted, few people entrenched in a gay lifestyle are going to change their behavior until they face a personal crisis, but thousands of people have left the gay lifestyle. This means, on the very face of it, that it is not immutable behavior. This is good news indeed; there is hope. Perhaps the reason so many young people are taking their own lives is because they feel hopeless. If you are a Christian, you have that hope inside you. Why not share it and declare it? Don't be silent! Speak out. Be kind, but don't back down from sharing. The stakes are high, and the next generation of our youth are at high risk.

The Moral Matrix

We are living in strange times when men can compete in women's sports . . . as women. Let me say right up front that this is anti-science, anti-God, anti-family, anti-woman, anti-everything that makes sense in the world. There are not seventy different genders. That I even need to write this seems preposterous. No, men cannot have babies. Yes, there are biological differences between men and women. These differences are not opinions; they are scientific facts. So why do we pretend otherwise?

So many have come to believe that any form of sexuality is perfectly fine, and that a promiscuous lifestyle, a homosexual lifestyle, or transgenderism are all just as good as a traditionally married and monogamous lifestyle. This is simply and plainly not true, as we will see shortly. When your kids were small, perhaps like mine, they liked to play make-believe. We knew it was just fantasy, spurred by an active imagination, and fun. But we did not allow them to stay there—as Batman or the Little Mermaid or some other animal or cartoon character. To do so would be allowing our children to grow up in a world of make-believe and therefore struggle with accepting reality. Yes, that is what we are dealing with today—make-believe. Pure fantasy.

In 1972, Title IX was passed, preventing sex-based discrimination in schools. It came on the heels of the Civil Rights Act but mainly gave women and girls a chance to compete athletically on a level playing field, opening up many more opportunities for them. However, what was designed to help women move forward has now been utterly demolished by transgender athletes, mostly males competing as females and largely wiping out women in their own sports. These women have trained for many years to reach a higher level of competition but are now in danger of being denied that higher level because men are entering women's sports. The recent high-profile case of a male swimmer who identifies as female started women's sports down a path that will be hard to undo.

Standing six-feet one-inch, Lia Thomas, born a male, decided to swim against women at Penn State; for the most part, he won. He then stood on the platform pretending to be a woman, taking medals away from biological women while pretending to be one of them. No regret. No remorse. Just make-believe. And the world stood by as more than half a century of protecting women in sports was systematically abolished by the LGBTQ propaganda machinery. The so-called defenders of women, of progressive politics, of feminism all sat by and did nothing.

Riley Gaines, a former University of Kentucky swimmer decided to speak up. "This is not progressive. We are not moving forward. This is actually quite the opposite. We're going back fifty years in time to before Title IX." A swimmer since she was age four, Gaines says, "If we as female athletes aren't willing to stick up for ourselves, we shouldn't expect someone else to stand up for us. Someone has to speak out truthfully. So I did." She said she felt like she was competing against Thomas with her hands tied behind her back. "We're watching the denial of the most basic of truths. When you can't acknowledge what a woman is, there's a huge problem," Gaines said. "This is deeper than just sports. This is a systematic erasure of what a woman is."[30]

Gaines, of course, has every right to be frustrated. The adults that protected her as a child, giving her a level playing field, suddenly failed when she needed that level field most. Women and girls are now forced to take action to protect their own sports by boycotting teams or players that have no business being there. These are players who are the opposite sex and yet share their locker rooms, stand on medal podiums to receive awards, and are treated as persecuted heroes. This needs to stop, and I believe it will when enough women rise up to protect their rightful place in sports and society.

Another story illustrates the problem even further, this one from the International Women's Day celebration where transgender Alba Rueda received the "Woman of Courage Award." The problem is that Rueda is a biological male who dresses like and pretends to be a woman. With the President's wife and the Secretary of State there to present the award, many Twitter followers mocked the absurdity of the escapade. Others suggested it was a mockery of women on a day women were supposed to be honored. The press release said the White House honored "11 extraordinary women from around the world who are working to build a brighter future for all."[31]

I have to wonder how honoring men pretending to be women help build a brighter future for girls and women. What does this convey to young girls? Perhaps you remember reading George Orwell's book *1984* during high school or college. Remember what it said.

- WAR IS PEACE
- FREEDOM IS SLAVERY
- IGNORANCE IS STRENGTH

It's the same playbook. Change the language. Ridicule and dismantle old values. Legislate new rules and shame those who protest them. And then there's the quote from the movie *The Matrix* when Neo asks, "Ever have that feeling you're not sure if you are awake or dreaming?" That's exactly where we are today. We watch as a gullible public pretends the emperor has clothes, when he's actually walking around as a naked fool thinking all is well. Someone must step forward and point out the obvious. Will you?

Orwell's fictional world is becoming our reality. Whatever the party holds as truth is truth. Power creates reality; it creates truth. This is dangerous territory! As theologian and author Os Guinness wrote in *Unriddling Our Times*, "Truth is essential to resist manipulation. If truth is dead and knowledge is power, then we are all vulnerable to passions and externally to manipulation . . . Truth is essential as a basis for freedom and fulfillment. Most people today view freedom only negatively—

freedom from authority and control."[32] Guinness goes on to observe that we are becoming accomplices to our own decline.

The Wizard Behind the Curtain

It was way back in 1987 when Professor Allan Bloom wrote a book called *The Closing of the American Mind.* He was prescient; he saw what would happen to our culture and the danger ahead if we didn't change course. He saw some of the signs I mentioned earlier that took place in the '60s and '70s. "Indiscriminate freedom," he said, "is the insatiable appetite to live as one pleases . . . the effective way to defang the oppressors is to persuade them they are ignorant of the good . . . There are no absolutes, freedom is absolute."[33]

Secularism, which fueled much of what we see today (remember our discussion of worldviews), is the belief that religion and religious consideration should be ignored. Religion must be set aside for the grander truths that science and intellect have to offer. It wasn't just Bloom who saw what was happening to culture. Former Supreme Court nominee Robert Bork made similar observations to our unrestrained hedonism. He noted that *social peace and cohesion decline as loneliness and alienation rise.* Think about that for a moment. Fifty-seven percent of teen girls feel persistently sad or hopeless. Is this not what we call an epidemic? One study found rampant sexual coercion and social media are fueling this sadness and hopelessness.[34]

We need to stop experimenting with kids' lives and futures. This is helping no one, let alone the kids who are suffering. Bork said in his book *Slouching Toward Gomorrah: Modern Liberalism and American Decline,* "The response of liberalism was not to turn to religion [for answers], which modernity had seemingly made irrelevant, but to abandon reason." [35] Both Bloom and Bork assert that liberalism and its permutations have sent us into a tailspin. These two authors sounded the alarm early on, somewhat like the proverbial canary in the coal mine, warning of impending disaster like Old Testament prophets. For the most part, their warnings went unheeded. As the prophet Joel wrote about people who cling to lies and refuse to accept truth, "They sow the wind and reap the whirlwind" (Hosea 8:7).

As I mentioned earlier, liberalism—now called progressivism—has sought God-less solutions to our greatest societal and personal challenges. It has relied instead on intuition, feelings, and of course, the science. No one seems to see the incompatibility between feelings and science, but that's best left for another discussion. What we do know is that married, monogamous, committed heterosexual relationships are the happiest and most stable.

If you will recall, the Wizard of Oz was exposed for the fraud he was by none less than a little dog by the name of Toto. We need to start playing Toto's role in our culture, in our community. Resisting lies means speaking out against them. Moral and scientific truth are the tools by which insanity is reigned in. Too many have been afraid, like the cowardly lion, to go out and face the great unknown. Courage means stepping into places and situations that may be uncomfortable for us. But be encouraged— you have moral high ground here. Never forget this.

Celebrating the Good

Sex is a gift from our Creator. He designed it, not just for pro-creation but for our enjoyment as well. Yes, God designed sex. It was His idea in the first place. Like all good gifts from our Creator, mankind seems to have a penchant for twisting and polluting it. Those who want to live without internal restraints on their behavior often deride those who choose a different path, meaning one of faithfulness and temperance. They want us to believe that because of our faith or values, we're missing out. But is this true? Are people in lifelong, monogamous heterosexual relationships miserable?

Marriage is good for our physical and emotional well-being. Married people are economically better off. Sex is better within marriage. Kids fare far better when parents are together, do better in school, have better future relationships, commit fewer crimes, stay in school, refrain from substance abuse, and are better off financially. That is not to say good marriages don't have their challenges; they clearly do. But overall, marriage is good, and divorce rarely offers the freedom we anticipate.

In *Second Chances*, Judith Wallerstein tells about the research she and her colleagues did on divorce. "We did not question the commonly held assumption that divorce was a short-lived crisis. But when we conducted follow-up interviews eighteen months later, we found most families still in crisis. Their wounds were wide open. Turmoil and distress had not noticeably subsided. Many adults still felt angry, humiliated, and rejected, and most had not gotten their lives back together. An unexpectedly large number of children were on a downward spiral. Their symptoms were worse than before. Their behavior at school was worse.

Their peer relationships were worse. Our findings were absolutely contradictory to our expectations."[36] Read that last line again. No, kids are not resilient when you upend their world. They hurt. They act out. They suffer. So why do we keep pretending that good marriages are a myth, that staying together is monotonous, or that absolute freedom is the holy grail?

What difference does marriage make? Do we really need a marriage license to prove anything? Isn't marriage an outdated patriarchal system? Let's look at the social benefits of traditional marriage. The social experimentation with marriage over the past decades is yielding a treasure trove of data. The alternatives to traditional marriage are an unqualified failure by every measure. The evidence clearly and unequivocally favors marriage. There is a clear link between marital status and personal well-being.

1. Married couples experience better physical and mental health. One theory posits this has to do with the coping, protecting, and support couples give one another.

2. Alcoholism is lower in married couples. The highest rate is among those who cohabited without ever marrying.

3. Suicide is lower in married couples. The highest rates of suicide are among the divorced, the widowed, and never married.

4. Marital status is a significant contributor to an individual's state of health and well-being. Married people suffer less from illness and disease and typically enjoy a longer life than those who are not married. Mortality rates in married people are lower.

5. Marriage discourages negative behaviors like smoking, excessive drinking, drug abuse, and other risky behaviors.
6. Married people enjoy significantly better mental health than those who are single, divorced, or separated.
7. Married people cope better with stress and depression. The theory is that marital partners provide emotional support and thereby reduce tension. [37]

In terms of self-reported levels of happiness and general well-being, married people are better off than non-married people. Marriage is God's idea. When we deviate from His design and purpose, we run into trouble. Kids are impacted. Society is impacted. Kids need moms *and* dads. I understand bad things happen in life and relationships, but the unmistakable truth is that marriage is good for us, good for kids, good for society, and healthier overall than non-marriage. Study after study reinforces the benefits for kids and all involved.

The next time someone drags out the old, tired argument about marriage being outdated or unimportant, tell them the truth. Debunk the confusion and lies about sex. Secularism has done untold damage to our society under the guise of personal freedom. But freedom without restraints is moral chaos, which is what we see all around us. As I said earlier, we are on strong moral ground here. Science and research support traditional sexuality and marriage. We can't have it both ways. Either good marriages build stronger societies, or they are harmful. Either alternative relationships are just as solid as traditional marriages, or they are not. Most important, we need to stop pretending in the equality of marriage with other relationship options.

When we devalue essential institutions like marriage or the definition of what healthy sexuality looks like, we soon find it easier to deceive ourselves into believing other untruths. One of these is the very essence of life and birth, as we will see in the next chapter.

CHAPTER FOUR

A Cult of Death: How Abortion Became a Religion

"Any country that accepts abortion is not teaching its people to love but to use violence to get what they want."
—Mother Teresa

C. Everett Koop served under President Ronald Reagan as Surgeon General of the United States during the 1980s. He said, "Eventually every nation in every age must be judged by this test: how did it treat people." I would take Dr. Koop's statement one step further: The way we treat the most vulnerable people in our society says much about the kind of people we are. Today, abortion is the most common medical procedure in the United States. By most estimates, we have slaughtered more than 60 million unborn babies since abortion was first legalized back in 1973 when the Supreme Court voted 7-2 in favor. As Westerners, we like to think majority rule is virtuous, but when you consider that majority rule led to the deaths of tens of millions of unborn, does this sound like a worthwhile moral value system? Sometimes the majority gets it wrong.

Abortion was the law of the land until Dobbs v. Jackson Women's Health Organization overturned the decision in 2022, holding the Constitution does not confer a right to abortion. Like the topic of sex and marriage in the previous chapter, abortion is one of the social-moral issues where progressives deliberately refuse to follow the science. Abortion has become a form of birth control for some women. It is seen by many as a personal right, a woman's right. I find this ironic because birth control was supposed to solve the problem of unwanted pregnancy. Clearly, it did not.

I do not intend to rehash the detail about how abortions are performed. A plethora of literature on the topic and methodology is readily available to any who wish to read it. But to put it mildly, abortion is nothing short of barbarism. It was Randall Terry who first started picketing abortion clinics with photos of hacked up or burned babies. While I am sure it may have dissuaded many women from having an abortion, the tool that played the biggest role—and still does—is ultrasound. This procedure is a window to the womb and enables women to hear their unborn child's heart beating and to see the hands, head, feet. No one can look at an ultrasound and deny this is a living, growing human being. To suggest otherwise is to abandon all science, reason, and morality.

As a person of deep faith, I find abortion repugnant. Plain and simple, it takes the life of a living, growing baby that has every right to live and thrive. If you are reading this and had an abortion in the past, as many have, I don't mean this as condemnation; rather, I want to extend hope and forgiveness to the many women who regret having such a procedure. However, abortion has consequences, and we will get into some of these later in the chapter. We can pretend this is simply a private issue, one that is exclusively about healthcare, but this is not true. Abortion is first and foremost a moral issue because it is the taking of an innocent life.

Western civilization has always taught the dignity of the individual and considered each person as unique. Jesus taught us the same. He empowered women. He encouraged them to make good choices. Some of those women were there for Him at the cross and were the first to show up at the empty tomb. And even in their day, this evil of infanticide was a very real practice. In fact, it has been around thousands of years, albeit for different reasons.

Molech and the Spirit of Death

Molech was an ancient god of the Canaanite people who lived in what is now modern-day Israel. Molech-worship is one of the reasons God instructed the Jews to destroy many of the people living in Canaan, but that is another story. Molech was made of bronze, had a bullish head and outstretched arms. The statue had an opening that allowed worshippers to build a fire inside. When the fire was hot enough, a child would be placed on the statue's outstretched arms and roasted alive. When the child screamed out in pain, priests beat drums to drown out the screams. I wonder if we would consider this practice barbaric today.

The Valley of Slaughter was an actual place outside the walls of Jerusalem. It was known by another name as well, Tophet or "fireplace," because parents sacrificed their children there. Two Jewish kings led the way in this abominable practice—Ahaz and Manasseh. God eventually judged His people for engaging in these pagan practices, speaking through the prophet Jeremiah: "[You] have filled this place with the blood of the innocent. [You] have built the high places of Baal to burn [your] children in the fire as offerings to Baal—something I did not command or mention, nor did it enter my mind" (Jeremiah 19:4,5). How is our culture any better than the pagan nations of the past?

English poet John Milton wrote about Molech in his classic *Paradise Lost*. Molech, he believed, was one of Satan's chief warriors and one of the fallen angels. God specifically told the Jews, "Do not follow their [Canaanites'] practices . . . Do not give any of your children to be sacrificed to [Molech], for you must not profane the name of your God. I am the LORD" (Leviticus 18:3, 21). God was the giver of life, and He forbade child sacrifice. His people were not to engage in the same practices as the cultures around them. They were to be separate (holy), have different laws and different values, a structure meant to put God first in their lives.

The worship of Molech was against everything God wanted for His people. The death of innocent children was not part of His plan. As Jesus said, "I have come that they may have life, and have it to the full" (John 10:10). But today, the spirit of Molech—child sacrifice—is alive and well in western civilization. I find this both tragic and ironic, since rationalism and ideas taken from the Enlightenment were supposed to save mankind, not destroy them or their offspring. Instead, by removing moral truth or the value of human life from the equation, western civilization soon found itself adrift in a sea of moral subjectivism. Nowhere is this more apparent than in our obsession with self-interest. Why do you think it is mostly people of faith who speak up for the rights of the unborn? Do people of faith care about self-interest? That is rhetorical. Unplanned pregnancies are not the sole domain of unbelievers. But the difference comes back to worldview. If we lack a worldview that places a high value on life, we will choose accordingly. None of this is new.

The worship of Molech started with the worship of sex and the sex goddess, Asherah, considered a fertility goddess. Followers often worshipped her through prostitution and ritual—sometimes even incestuous—sexual practice. In other words, ritual sex was one way people worshipped this goddess. Are you starting to see the connection between aberrant sexuality and child sacrifice? In those days, the land was scattered with Asherah poles shaped in the form of phallic symbols. God detested these practices because they polluted the land and the people, and destroyed families. Sadly, Molech worship is alive and well in our world today, though we have created far more sophisticated means of destroying human life. In some cases, we even celebrate it, which seems even more barbaric. The signs at pro-abortion rallies read, "Abortion is healthcare," "Abortion Saves Lives," or "Shout Your Abortion." Imagine the level of callousness and self-deception it takes to equate removing a living child from one's womb to *saving* life or *healthcare*? I also find the euphemism "pro-choice" another deception, since it only involves choice for one person: the woman choosing to abort her child. Though getting an abortion is more difficult in some states today, it remains readily available in others. If Planned Parenthood has its way, abortion will be easier and less difficult to obtain than ever before.

"Let's Get Started"

Cecile Richards, a former president of Planned Parenthood, started an abortion chatbot called Charley that helps women who want to end their pregnancies. Charley's website greets visitors with the message, "Need an abortion? Let's get started." The left has gone from making abortion safe and rare to making it easy and often. According to Nicole Cushman, Charley's New York-based content manager, their stated goal is to "meet abortion seekers whenever they are online." This is Planned Parenthood's response to the overturning of Roe v. Wade. It's called a "workaround," a way to get the job done regardless of the obstacles, or as Cushman says, to "improve people's online search experience." This is how evil operates, by finding creative ways to destroy life, all in the name of education or healthcare. This is precisely what Satan tries to do: package evil and rebellion as nicely as possible, making good seem wrong and bad seem good. It replaces life with death by elevating personal choice above moral truth. The abortion proponents refer to this as "compassionate and comprehensive care, especially as something so personal as an abortion."[38]

Losing Our Religion

Why do I refer to abortion as a form of religion? Here is one of the definitions of religion: *Cause, principle, or system of beliefs held to with ardor and faith.*

This definition fits most pro-abortionists. But what exactly is their focus of worship? It comes down to one thing: self-interest. This takes many forms, of course, but words like *convenience* dominate the belief system. When convenience predominates, it must be accompanied by a moral-value system and a sense of personal rights. Pro-abortion advocates have both, leading to an ends-justify-the-means conclusion, which comes directly from humanist philosophy. Moral right is determined by majority vote. The Judeo-Christian tradition gets in the way of personal freedom by going beyond the individual. It includes, among other considerations, the unborn and the community. When man is at the center of all things and there is no God, people determine their own truth—or what they think is right or wrong based on what they feel works best for themselves and their circumstances. It is subjective morality.

As Francis Schaeffer wrote four decades ago, "The freedom that was once founded on biblical consensus and a Christian ethos has now become autonomous freedom." He goes on to say, "All morality becomes relative, law becomes arbitrary, and society moves toward disintegration. In personal and social life, compassion is swallowed up by self-interest."[39]. Morality cannot be based on self-interest or consensus. Do you see how this can be a slippery slope when individuals or a society adopt such values? These can change at the wishes or whims of cultural elites. This is exactly what happened during World War II when

Hitler made the following grandiose statement: "As the last factor I must name my own person in all modesty: irreplaceable. Neither a military man nor a civilian could replace me . . . I am convinced of the powers of my intellect and of decision . . . No one has ever achieved what I have achieved . . . I have led the German people to great height, even if the world does hate us now."[40] Hitler was his own little god. He made his own rules. He decided who should live and who should die . . . as do abortionists. Hitler acted out on a worldview entrenched in humanism and bolstered by the Germans' collective inferiority complex. People like Dietrich Bonhoeffer spoke up and encouraged church leaders to push back. Some did; most did not.

Theologian Schaeffer said, "Without a firm set of principles that flows out of a world-view that gives an adequate reason for a unique value to all human life, there cannot be and will not be any substantial resistance by the present evil brought on by the low view of human life . . . the humanist world-view has brought us to the present devaluation of human life." [41] Is it any wonder a generation of young people are growing up depressed, addicted, and hopeless? If life has no meaning and there is no future, what's the purpose of life and living? If people keep hearing the same refrain—that personal choice is the preeminent virtue and all else is expendable—why not their lives too?

During the latter half of the twentieth century, a tiny five-foot tall Albanian Catholic nun became a prominent figure in the prolife movement. Mother Teresa devoted her life to help those who could not help themselves on the streets of Calcutta, India. She never intended to be a political lightening rod, though at times she was. She had no interest in money, fame, or doing much except reaching out to the helpless. Mother Teresa once said, "Human rights are not a privilege conferred by government. They are every human being's entitlement by virtue of his humanity. The right to life does not depend, and must not be contingent, on the pleasure of anyone else, not even a parent or sovereign . . . You must weep that your own government, at present, seems blind to this truth."[42]

Truth? Who's truth? What truth? Who determines this truth? One of the great tragedies of our time is that we have allowed a shape-shifting truth to infect our culture. Make no mistake—this cult of death is destroying our very soul and the souls of our children. But does this pro-abortion belief system have any consequences to the adherents who give allegiance to it?

An Inconvenient Truth

We are told that abortion sets a woman free. It liberates her, frees her from a certain economic privation, gives her a new lease on life, a chance to finish school or avoid stigmatization. For decades, abortion clinics told women they were removing the elements of conception, a tumor, or a blob of tissue, assuring them it was not a real baby; it was not viable, could not live on its own. Therefore, as the logic goes, it was worthless—unless the aborted fetal neuronal cells can be used to treat Parkinson's or Huntington's disease or for certain vaccines that we were told might save lives. In any field of science, we know something that is living and growing is not dead or failing to move toward life. When individual convenience trumps common sense or science, as it does in many areas today, we are on a fast path to losing touch with objective reality.

There is more to this abortion business than the unborn victim. The woman who chooses abortion often faces a life-long struggle to free herself—wittingly or unwittingly—from a mental or spiritual prison of anguish. The inconvenient truth is one many women who have had an abortion know all too well—Post Abortion Syndrome (PAS). This is the experience no one wants to talk about, especially those at abortion clinics.

According to therapist Teri Reisser, "The instinct to protect and nurture the child growing within is 'hard-wired.'" When a woman has an abortion, she uses various coping strategies to convince herself the decision is right, or good, or necessary. But according to Reisser, these internal excuses often spill out, sometimes years later. The impact of PAS can be debilitating and includes:

- Guilt
- Anxiety
- Depression
- PTSD effects (re-experiencing events related to abortion)
- Fertility, pregnancy, and bonding issues
- Survivor guilt
- Self-abusive or self-destructive behaviors
- Anniversary reactions
- Brief psychotic disorder

"Most post-abortion women carry an 'abortion wound' in their hearts but have never specifically identified it or understood its ongoing impact," says Reisser. "They carried their secrets like a heavy chain around their heart . . . they felt not only defective but also extremely reluctant to broach this subject for fear of being judged." [43]

Think about this for a moment. Most estimates say between 25 and 40 percent of American women have had an abortion. This represents somewhere between 42 and 70 million women. The residual impact from these abortions is enormous. Depression, anxiety, PTSD, substance abuse, and mental disorders in women have increased by as much as 20 percent. I am convinced many—though certainly not all—the women who struggle with guilt or shame carry it like a heavy ball and chain. They feel the impact of their decision even if they cannot pinpoint the exact reasons. There is no other explanation for the rapid deterioration of women's mental health. We don't see this information in most literature on the topic because the pain women carry is often hidden, kept quiet, internalized, or compartmentalized. Abortion does not end all of a woman's problems as the abortion industry wants us to believe. It simply transfers the problems elsewhere.

Yes, All Lives Matter

Inconvenient truths are everywhere. The question is, why are these truths ignored by the mainstream media or the progressives? For example, did you know that one in three Black babies are aborted in this country? If we are serious about Black lives mattering, why so little conversation about abortion? Does it strike you a bit odd that nearly 80 percent of Planned Parenthood clinics are in Black and minority neighborhoods? [44]

Let me be clear about God's view of life. All lives matter to Him, and because all lives matter to Him, they should matter to us as well. This means born and unborn. Young and old. Black and White. Handicapped and whole. If He cares about the widows and orphans, how much more does He care about the unborn? He is the Author of Life. We are made in His image and likeliness. This truth gives value to human life. Abortion is not just an individual issue. It is not a feminist issue. It isn't even a religious issue. It is a human issue. Author Os Guinness believes that past civilizations and empires are brought down by sin within the society ... and the passing of time, since no human success lasts forever. America is being wrecked foremost by the presence of sin, which diminishes the intrinsic value of human life. If we agree—and we should—that Black lives matter, then all other lives matter as well. To live as if they do not is to violate the very nature of being.

Dr. Brian Haynes gave us a glimpse into the uniqueness of humanity when he said, "Humans are the only beings created in the image of God. When the adversary looks into the face of a man, woman, boy, or girl, he sees the image of God. We are a constant reminder to Satan of the glory of the Most High God ... He hates us and this is why he relentlessly attacks us in both general and specific ways. The enemy desires human brokenness, disconnection from the truly loving God, destruction of marriage and family, and eternal damnation of our souls."[45] The destruction of that which matters most to God is part of Satan's plan. And his name means adversary or one who resists. His goal is to oppose what God wants—a close relationship with mankind. Naturally, the enemy will do all he can to destroy human life—before birth, in the womb, or after birth through drugs, abuse, suicide—it does not matter how he gets the job done. But in no place is he more effective than by eradicating babies from being born—and no one is more cunning at creating deception.

The Lies We Are Told

Joseph Goebbels was Adolph Hitler's Minister of Public Enlightenment and Propaganda. He said, "The most brilliant propagandist technique will yield no success unless one fundamental principle is borne in mind constantly—it must confine itself to a few points and repeat them over and over."[46] I want you to think for a moment how this same technique is being used in Western culture today. Here are a few examples.

- A fetus is simply a blob of tissue; it is not a human being.
- Gays are born that way.
- Only women have the right to choose when to end a pregnancy.
- Surgery can change a person's gender.
- Human life does not begin until birth.
- Abortion is often the best choice for a woman.

The list goes on, but you have no doubt heard this *ad infinitum* in one form or another. They are all lies, of course, but we hear them as truths, repeated as if they were commonly known to be fact. The voices of people like Mother Teresa or Viktor Frankl should serve as a warning that when we destroy human life, we destroy a part of ourselves. It was Frankel who said, ". . . human life, under any circumstances, never ceases to have meaning."[47] We cannot reinvent the truth to suit our present circumstances, no matter how dire they may be at any given moment.

What we see happening across cultures today is massive, collective, corporate self-deception. The more we hear lies, the more we tend to accept them. That is why standing up for truth is so vital, especially now. If we do not, we succumb to the lies we are told. This is not just about abortion. You and I must speak up in all areas of truth. Let your voice be heard. Be kind but firm. The self-deception begins when we rationalize and justify what we know to be wrong. We make excuses, such as, "It's not really a human being yet." But we know it is. Deep inside, every woman who is carrying a baby knows there is new life growing inside of her. How could she know otherwise?

The process of rationalizing is nothing new. Adam used it in the Garden of Eden when he blamed his wrong choices on Eve, and Eve in turn blamed the serpent. It is easy to see how other people rationalize but harder to look at ourselves, our nation, or our family. "It's just not the same," we reason. "You don't understand my circumstances," or "God doesn't judge; He's all about love and acceptance." Our compromise, our excuses, our rationalization does not change the truth. We know excuses around abortion can be compelling, so let's not ignore the big ones.

First, what about abortion in the case of rape or incest? Does being prolife mean a woman cannot terminate a pregnancy in such awful circumstances? Let's start by agreeing on this: rape is evil. Rape must be punished. Rape is a violation of a woman in the most intimate way. Incest is evil. It too must be punished. A father, stepfather, uncle, or sibling who violates a family member—girl, woman, or boy—should suffer the consequences of their sinful choices. Let me be clear. When anyone is forced into a sexual act against their will, it is wrong. No excuse. Period. But the answer to the second half of this question regarding permission to terminate a pregnancy resulting from rape or incest is what we often get wrong. Isn't the unborn child also a victim if the mother decides to abort the child? Is the unborn child, regardless of how he or she was conceived, not also made in the image of God? To be prolife means not making exceptions when the termination of human life is in question.

When life begins, even in the worst of circumstances, it remains life. Rape and incest are a tragic part of our fallen and sin-wrecked world. They are symptomatic of brokenness and evil. But we do not punish outcomes; we punish evildoers—or should. We do not punish the unborn; we punish evildoers—or should. We have come to see feelings as a viable marker for moral decision-making when they clearly are not. Feelings are fickle. Feelings can be inaccurate. Feelings can be manipulated.

And we have a final question, commonly posed as a way to prove abortion can be an act of mercy: What about abortion in the case of deformity or severe handicap? When author Nancy Guthrie's daughter Hope was born, the new parents were quickly informed that something was wrong. Doctors informed them that several little things were not quite right with Hope, warning of the presence of a deeper, more serious problem. Not long after Hope's birth and diagnosis, Nancy became pregnant again. This time she was told her second child had Zellweger Syndrome, a rare genetic disorder for which there is no treatment. What would you do in such a heart-wrenching situation, particularly if doctors may advise you to terminate the pregnancy? This godly couple chose to take both babies to term, then loved and nurtured them the best they could, knowing they would not live full lives.

There are countless people who have struggles and limitations in life. Some of these are physical or mental. Walt Disney was dyslexic. Albert Einstein was autistic. Beethoven and Thomas Edison were mostly deaf. Franklin Roosevelt was crippled by polio. Helen Keller was deaf and blind. Nick Vujicic was born without arms or legs and is a motivational speaker today. Dr. John Nash, from the movie *A Beautiful Mind,* was a paranoid schizophrenic. Stephen Hawking suffered from ALS (Amyotrophic Lateral Sclerosis). My question is this: Which of these contributors to our society should not have been given the chance to make the most of their limitations in life?

Let's end this chapter about human life with the words of theologian Os Guinness. ". . . The cleverer the mind, the more slippery the heart. The more sophisticated the education, the subtler the rationalization. Sometimes erudition only lends conviction to self-deception, for no one is easier to deceive than ourselves."[48]

CHAPTER FIVE

Why Defunding Police Is Societal Suicide

"A distinctive feature of modern liberalism is its unwillingness to deal with crime with the rigor it deserves and that the general public wants."
—Robert H. Bork

When Nashville Police Officers Rex Engelbert and Michael Collazo got the call about an active shooter at Covenant School in Nashville, they didn't hesitate to jump into action. The shooter, twenty-eight-year-old Audrey Hale, had carefully planned the assault, bringing significant ammunition and three weapons to the attack: two semiautomatic rifles and a handgun. Hale ultimately shot 152 rounds inside the Christian school. Bodycam footage showed the officers methodically going from room to room looking for the shooter. Once they located Hale, they ended the nightmare that took the lives of three nine-year-olds and three adults who worked at the school. As more detail came to light, the sad truth emerged that Hale was "hunting the pastor who had counseled her." She couldn't find Pastor Chad Scruggs, so she decided to shoot his nine-year-old daughter, Hallie, instead.

Gun Control ... or Heart Change?

Gun-control activist and Audrey's mom, Norma Hale, had previously posted about keeping guns out of schools. Her daughter identified as a transgender, having been born female but going by he/him pronouns. The reference to Norma's "daughter" was at odds with the mass killer's LinkedIn profile using "he/him" pronouns and at times using the male name Aiden. Norma had previously requested Congress make large-capacity gun magazines illegal. She shared another petition titled "Keep Guns Out of Schools." According to Nashville police chief, John Drake, the shooting suspect had considered striking two locations but chose the Covenant School because it had less security. Ironically and tragically, Norma Hale knew Audrey had purchased a gun well before the mass shooting occurred, yet her gun-control activism had zero outcome on the mass murder committed by her daughter. We now know the shooter had purchased seven guns and was under a doctor's care for an emotional disorder. She reached out to a friend earlier and said, "I just need to die." Premediated. Callous. Violent. Senseless. Evil.

What's my point in telling you this story? If police were unarmed or unavailable, how many more children and adults might have died without the brave and decisive actions of officers Engelbert and Collazo? Sure, we can defund the police because we think they are the problem, but doing so only creates a new set of problems, including emboldening criminals and empowering those with mental illness. And yes, I think many of these young transgenders with autism need psychiatric help, not scalpels to fix what ails them most. Regardless, let's stop pretending the police are the problem in this country.

What about hormone treatments, advocated by transgender-affirming advocates? We should learn about potential hormone-doping risks—risks that should frighten patients, their parents, and a society committed to so-called "compassion and safety." One of the risks for women of testosterone-doping is increased aggression. Was Hale, who used the pronouns "he/him," testosterone-doping? What leads me to suspect this may be the case? It is simply this fact: female mass murderers are extremely rare.

Cultural analyst and author Matt Barber had suspicions early-on that the Nashville school murders involved an anti-Christian attack incited by an LGBTQ mindset. Sadly, it turned out Barber was right. As stated above Audrey Hale was a so-called transgender—a woman who identified as a man—with a grudge against a particular Christian pastor. When she went looking for him but couldn't find him, she instead killed nine others at a Christian school, including three children. Sounds like a hate crime to me.

An image of transgender activist Kayla Denker, who goes by "Pinko Scum," shows him loading and racking an AR-15, with a caption that reads "while advocating for trans people to 'arm ourselves' is not any of a solution to the genocide we're facing . . . if you transphobes do try to come for me I'm taking a few of you with me." Signs reading "Trans rights or else," with various automatic weapons between the words, are part of trans rallies. In one Tweet, a transgender individual with an AR-15 and a handgun is pictured along with the words "Kill christ-cucks. Behead christcucks," and "Crucify filthy christcucks," as well as "slam dunk a christcuck baby into a trashcan." The post is hash-tagged "trans day of vengeance."[49] You can make your own determination about what all of this means. I believe people of faith who want to be left alone to raise their children without interference and indoctrination are quickly becoming the targets of violent, mentally-ill people desperate for acceptance. This is what our families, our police, and our schools are dealing with on a regular basis.

It didn't take twenty-four hours after the shooting in Tennessee before progressives once again pointed out the need for gun control. Hollywood actress Jana Kramer wrote on her Instagram, "My heart is absolutely breaking for the children and the families right now. Why. Why. Why. I just will never understand." Another actress named Jane Lynch posted, "We live in a world where it has become acceptable to shoot children dead in school." Actress Katie Stevens, who just gave birth to her first child, wrote, "Weeping for the families who don't get to hold their babies again. I will never understand why this keeps happening. And why children are dying because our country is failing to put laws in place that protect them . . . The fact that there are laws to 'protect' children from drag queens and not gun violence is INFURIATING to me."

I feel their pain. It is nauseating. Really. But as I said earlier, we all want to see changes, but we never make the *right* ones. Let me be clear; it is not gun-registered hunters who go around schools killing children. Progressives can get as mad as they want—and in some instances, we all should. But this is not about guns; this is about the human heart. This is about a deep brokenness in our own society, one that is becoming embedded. The same people who scream "shout your abortion" are the ones who suddenly become purveyors of moral truth and wannabe protectors of innocent life taken in a school shooting. Do you see the irony? This had nothing to do with protecting children from drag shows, which we wholeheartedly ought to do. Rather, it has to do with teaching our children that human life matters because God says it does.

Jesus Ayala, eighteen, and Jazamir Keys, sixteen, stole a car in Las Vegas. It wasn't their first offense. After three car thefts and three hit-and-runs, they thought it would be amusing to intentionally run down a former Southern California police chief when they spotted him riding his bicycle. Andy Probst, sixty-four, was taken to University Medical Center where he was pronounced dead. The teens did not even stop at the scene. Police identified Keys as the passenger who recorded the incident while both teens laughed. The two face charges of murder, attempted murder, battery with use of a deadly weapon, leaving the scene of an accident, and numerous larceny and burglary charges. Keys's mother said, "My son's side of the story will be told, 'the truth,' not the inaccuracies the media will try to portray." When the police caught the two fugitives, Ayala told the arresting officer, "You think this juvenile [expletive] is gonna do some [expletive]? I'll be out in 30 days. I'll bet you. It's just ah, [expletive], hit-and-run—slap on the wrist."[50] Respect for human life? None. Respect for the police? None. Respect for the justice system? None. Never mind this woman's son just mowed down a retired policeman; she decided her son was somehow being misunderstood. This brazen disrespect is without excuse. Yet we continue to see woke politicians who place the blame everywhere except on their own inane polices.

Charles Colson wrote in *Kingdoms in Conflict*, "The view that man in his own rational interest can sustain a man-made religion is voiced regularly . . . It remains fashionable because it offers a positive view of human nature, filled with hopeful optimism about man's capacities. But it ignores a ringing testimony of a century filled with terror and depravity." The positivist mindset is humanism. The Bible teaches that man is irretrievably broken without God's redemptive effort through Jesus. Humanism teaches than man is slowly evolving and will get better, that religion is the problem, not disbelief in God. As Colson said, "The influence of the Kingdom of God in the public arena is good for society as a whole."[51]

Moral Chaos and Societal Disintegration

Hillary Ronen is a Democrat who represents District 9 on the San Francisco Board of Supervisors. In 2020, Ronen declared, "I want to make it clear that I believe strongly in defunding the police and reducing the number of officers on our force. For decades we've had an imbalance in our city's budget, with hundreds of millions of dollars going to SFPD to have them do work they are not qualified to do." The mayor then redirected $120 million from law enforcement to fund other city initiatives.

Progressive idealism recognizes few boundaries. You can guess what happened after their grand experiment was put into action in San Francisco. Crime worsened. Homicide increased by 20 percent in the first year and nearly that much the following year. In summary, their experiment did not work; it actually made the city worse. Ronen attacked the police chief for spending a large amount of overtime on an anti-retail theft program instead of prioritizing police presence in her district. "I have been begging this department to give the Mission District what it deserves in terms of police presence all year long. I have been told time and time and time again there are no officers that we can send to the Mission District." Yes, that's what happens when a city decides to defund the police. Why could Ronan not see the possibilities of her own policies? "It hurts" said Ronen. "And I feel betrayed by my department. I feel betrayed by the mayor. I feel betrayed by the priorities of the city."[52] After defunding the police, these progressives now believe they are the victims, not the people they are supposed to serve.

The so-called reimagining of public safety has increased crime, put police at risk, and led to fear among law-abiding citizens. Let's look at a few progressive cities to see how defunding police is playing out in real life.

- **Minneapolis**: Following the death of George Floyd and the resulting civil unrest, the Minneapolis City Council unanimously approved a budget that shifted approximately $8 million from the police department toward violence prevention and other programs. As a result, between the end of 2020 and early 2023, the homicide rate rose 46 percent. Violent crime is up 22 percent year after year. Money was diverted from the police budget to cover mental-health teams. Several groups, including city council members, wanted to disband the police altogether.

- **Portland:** The city made massive police budget cuts in 2020. City commissioners voted to cut nearly $16 million from the police budget in response to concerns about use of force and racial injustice. Homicides quickly skyrocketed 270 percent compared to the same time the previous year. The city saw a 1600 percent increase in murders in 2021 alone. Businesses were targeted by looters, vandals, and thieves. What was left of the decimated police department was unable to respond to calls for help. Protesters and rioters, many of them from Antifa, marched in Portland streets, demanding change and an end to racism. The unrest was often violent and destructive and, in many instances, targeted law enforcement officers and facilities. Portland redirected their law-enforcement budget to gun reduction, school resource officers, and social-service programs.

- **Austin:** The Austin City Council unanimously voted to cut roughly one-third of the city's $434 million police budget, slashing just over $150 million. The funds were designated to be redirected to social services. The cuts eliminated 150 open jobs. Aggravated assault reports were up 26 percent the year after Austin reduced the force. One of the reasons for the rise in homicides, according to the acting chief of police, relates to current staffing issues at Austin Police Department. "The fewer officers I have on patrol, it is going to impact that. And, I think that has played a part in this overall increase we're seeing in the numbers of murders and aggravated assaults."[53] Those in favor of defunding police will never admit to the obvious: that crime increases as police presence decreases. The blame is always the same—the availability of guns.

- **Los Angeles**: City leaders voted to cut the Los Angeles Police Department budget by $150 million, reducing the number of officers to a level not seen for more than a decade. About two-thirds of the funding was earmarked for police overtime and was instead used to provide services and programs for communities of color, including a youth summer-jobs program. The first year after the decision, the murder rate increased by 28 percent. The number of shooting victims nearly doubled, and aggravated assaults were up by more than 8 percent.

- **New York**: The New York City Council voted to move $1 billion away from the NYPD's budget and instead use it for education and social services. The cuts came from canceling a nearly 1,200-person police recruiting class, halving overtime spending, redeploying officers from administrative functions to patrol, and ending police responsibility for school-crossing guards and homeless outreach. The police department gave up control over public-school security. You can guess what happened next. Murders in New York City went up 11.8 percent.

The number of shootings rose 40 percent, and the number of shooting victims jumped 39 percent.[54]

So reads the tale of five cities with mayors and city council members who thought defunding the police was the ticket to a better, safer, and more loving society. They thought by defunding the police it would mysteriously provide the solution to gun violence, school shootings, police brutality, inequity, and racism. This magical thinking presupposes that if you treat people lovingly, they will respond accordingly. This is the fallacy of a humanist worldview. Criminologists spent many decades trying a rehabilitation model that was supposed to make criminal offenders want to rejoin society and be good boys and girls. Millions of tax dollars went into this model until the notion was mostly abandoned. Here we are again, seeing it happen with our hard-working police.

Defunding Fallout

The recidivism rate (re-arrest rate) for violent criminals is about 64 percent. Two-thirds of all violent offenders will kill, rape, or maim again. This isn't my opinion; this is based on government statistics. The rate is twice as high as it is for non-violent offenders. What does this tell us? That there are bad people in the world who do not care about your feelings. They do not care about your family or about doing the right thing. And they certainly do not care about making changes in their own lives.

Progressives do not think we should label people because this makes them *feel* bad. They insist labeling might perpetuate their criminal behavior. The solution? Change the language because that will fix everything. We are not to call people felons; we are to call them "justice-involved people." Progressives are attempting to erase words like offender or addict. An addict is now a "person with a history of substance abuse." Instead of shackling an underaged criminal with the label of juvenile delinquent, we call them a "young person with justice-system involvement."

Think for a moment just how ludicrous this sanitized and senseless language is starting to sound. A person whose car has been broken into could well be known to police as "a person who has come in contact with a returning resident who was involved with the justice system and has a history of substance use and is currently under supervision." Are you kidding? Imagine a rapist goes to a "camp," which used to be known as a prison. He gets out and tells a prospective employer that he is a "justice-impacted person." The illegal immigrant says he's a "person seeking lawful status." He is not an illegal alien because that is too dehumanizing. For criminals, progressives warn, the process is dehumanizing, debasing, and derogatory. Never mind there is a victim out there somewhere who has been killed, raped, robbed, or abused. This is what I mean by societal disintegration. It is ludicrous to think behavior is changed by altering the terminology or downsizing police departments. Behavior changes only if and when a person determines to change it, not before. Not with new semantics. Not by counseling. Not even through incarceration. In fact, incarceration is not to make people better, as it sometimes makes them worse. Prison is to protect law-abiding citizens from bad people. And it is not the police's job to make people better; their job is to protect and serve.

Who are the biggest losers in all this nonsense? We are. The law-abiding citizens who want to live our lives in peace, love our kids, and be left alone. Clearly, the correlation between defunding police departments and crime is obvious to anyone who chooses to see it, and it is not a complicated correlation. Not surprisingly, some of the same cities that chose to follow the movement and redirect or defund their resources have suddenly realized it was a bad idea. They did it because of a visceral reaction to images they saw of George Floyd with a White cop's knee on him. Suddenly, everything was about race, about the police, about inequity. The media fanned the flames, pretending cops were the problem instead of the people who run from the cops, ignore their warnings, or disrespect them. Let's look at this premise for a moment.

Teach Your Children Well

Philadelphia District Attorney Larry Krasner has been a harsh critic of the criminal-justice system and campaigned on a platform of radical reforms. The DA's victory party featured chants of "F--k the police" and "No good cops in a racist system." When you have this kind of reckless rhetoric, a growing tension between the public and the police is inevitable. Police across the country are labeled racist, arrogant, or abusive. Assaults against police jumped 20 percent from 2014 to 2017, up to about 60,000 a year, and this was before things got even worse in our country.[55]

Sgt. Christopher Brewster of the Houston Police Department was shot and killed while responding to a domestic-violence call, often the most dangerous calls police have to take. Several hours later that same day, Officer Stephen Carr of Arkansas's Fayetteville Police Department was ambushed and executed while sitting in his patrol vehicle.[56] A week later, Detective Joseph Seals was shot and killed by those who carried out the Jersey City massacre. Children in public schools are certainly at risk, but how much greater the risk for a cop in a blue state or city.

In the last two decades, the number of police per capita has dropped 11 percent. An obvious assumption might be that crime is going down; sadly, that's not the case. So what's behind the growing animosity toward the police and, more importantly, what can be done about it? I believe the two most important reasons police are under attack have to do with the disintegration of the family and media portrayals of bad cops. We learn respect in our family. This includes respect for parents, for teachers, for the law, for law enforcement, and even for God. Without respect, each of these systems is put at risk. I would go so far as to say, if we don't show respect for our parents, we certainly won't show respect for the police. Former students walking into a school and killing people starts with disrespect.

There is a reason God gave us a fifth commandment: "Honor your father and mother, so that you may live long in the land the LORD your God is giving you" (Exodus 20:12). Honor is just another word for respect. When God gave that commandment, He knew that without respect for parents, society is doomed. I hear parents tell me all the time how difficult it is to enforce discipline with their kids, whether it is calling for a time-out or taking away some social media privileges or gaming. These parents act as if they have no control within their own home or with their own children. And, of course, I understand that being a single parent makes the job even more difficult. But remember, the respect children show outside the home begins with their respect for parents inside the home.

A society that elevates personal autonomy above family or community interests is a society destined to fall. Right here, right now, here in America, we're doing exactly that, and we're seeing the signs of crumbling. When the very people who are there to protect us are under attack, good people must stand in the gap to encourage, support, and speak out. The fifth commandment was designed to place family and community above the individual. Why? Because when individuals are allowed to do as they please, this selfish and rebellious behavior infects the family or the community, much like cancer. Criminals are, in fact, a cancer to law-abiding citizens and a community. As researcher Robert Bellah observed, "The American understanding of the autonomy of the self places the burden of one's own deepest self-definitions on one's own individual self." In *Habits of the Heart*, Bellah went on to say, "Most of us imagine an autonomous self existing independently, entirely outside any tradition and community."[57] Bellah, speaking nearly forty years ago, saw what was coming. His observation of the impact of the individualism of the '60s and '70s concerned him. His own research showed the beginning signs of limitless autonomy and how it often leads to rebellion.

When young people grow up without respect, they later show none when they encounter the police. This is a reality few talk about but police will affirm. Criminals show no respect when they break the law, nor do they show any when they are asked to comply with the police's basic orders. A child that grows up on the religion of "me first, all others after" will act according to his own self-interests. If he's pulled over for speeding, he becomes angry or disrespectful because he has been inconvenienced. He may smart off or even use his cellphone to try and get the police to respond so he can become a famous TikTok star or post the video on Facebook or Instagram. The police put up with this kind of nonsense all the time. Instead of complying with an officer's commands, a criminal may run, fight back, or try to steal an officer's gun. Is it any wonder, when police feel their lives are at stake, they make split-second decisions to protect themselves, their partner, or the community? Do they ever get it wrong? Of course. Police must deal with domestic violence, drug addicts, mentally ill persons, rioters, and dangerous felons; they conduct wellness checks, do traffic stops, then write it all down. In every situation, they are expected to get it right *every single time.* No other job expects this kind of perfection.

Silencing Detractors

Sakira Cook is the senior director of the justice-reform program at The Leadership Conference on Civil and Human Rights. She is one of many voices pushing for reducing or eliminating police. "For decades, policymakers have pushed tough-on-crime policies that have not made us safer, but only wreaked havoc and destroyed lives—particularly in Black and Brown communities, while costing us billions," Cook said. She went on to say that tough-on-crime officials often implement strict criminal codes, long prison sentences, and expanded police power on the streets.[58]

Contrary to Cook's false statements, the most serious crime-ridden areas of the U.S. are Black and Brown communities—Baltimore, Detroit, St. Louis, Little Rock, Cleveland, Stockton, and Albuquerque. The best thing we can do to help our brothers and sisters of color is to show them we care by protecting their law-abiding citizens from criminals.

When Rudy Giuliani was mayor of New York City, he was tough on crime. When he took office, the city was called "ungovernable." It was too big, the problems too complicated. Under his conservative leadership, however, the city went from being a crime capitol to becoming America's safest big city. This was no accident or coincidence, but rather it is what happened when a serious-minded police-supporting mayor encouraged rather than discouraged NYPD. The violent crime rate dropped by 56 percent during the eight years Giuliani served as mayor. Murder was down nearly two-thirds, robbery down 67 percent, aggravated assault down 28 percent.

Justice reformers like Cook need to read their history books if they want safe communities. Giuliani brought confidence to a police force that felt besieged and demoralized under the previous Democratic administration. Howard Safir, the city's police commissioner from 1996 to 2000, said Giuliani deserves the credit because he provided leadership and badly needed support. "When I left it was the safest large city in America. You don't do that by not aggressively enforcing the laws," Giuliani said.[59]

If we cannot learn from what works, how will we ever learn from what does not work? It all comes down to respect for our police, love for our neighbors, and teaching respect in home and school. Tough-on-crime policies *do* work; to say otherwise is a lie. And to defund police is to put communities at risk.

CHAPTER SIX

Character, Color, and Systemic Dependency

"People, I just want to say, you know, can we, can we all get along? Can we get along?"
—Rodney King

O n March 3, 1991, Rodney King became a household name. A Black man on parole for robbery, King was drunk and running from the police. He was finally caught and brutally beaten by four police officers, three of whom were White. They used tasers, feet, and fists, leaving King with skull fractures, broken bones and teeth, and permanent brain damage. The officers were charged with excessive use of force, and rightfully so.

The National Guard was called in to bring order to the riots that followed King's beating. In the end, more than sixty people died in the melee, more than 2,300 were injured, and roughly 12,000 were arrested. The destruction to property, mostly in Black neighborhoods, included 1,000 buildings; the overall estimated damage was $1 billion.[60]

When the riots got out of hand, it was Rodney King himself who stepped in during a press conference and encouraged an end to the violence. "We all can get along. We've just got to stop. You know, I mean, we're all stuck here for a while. Let's, you know, let's try to work it out. Let's try to work it out."

Rodney King was not the first Black man to be brutalized; sadly, he won't be the last. As I said in the previous chapter, the police do not always get it right, but most of the time they do. Would King have been brutally beaten had he stopped after being signaled to do so rather than trying to flee? This is pure conjecture, but my best guess is that the police would not have treated him so severely if he had not tried to escape. He endangered many people by fleeing the police that day, as is often the case when someone runs rather than comply with the police. While this is in no way a justification for excessive police actions, different choices on King's part would likely have changed the outcome, especially for the other sixty people who died needlessly.

Fanning the Flames of Dependence

Have you ever stood next to a fire and seen the red embers glowing? The flames start to wane, but the heat still comes from the embers. If you pick up a piece of cardboard and start fanning the fire, what happens? It roars back to life. This is a metaphor for what is happening in our country now. People deliberately fan the embers of hate and violence, trying to make our great nation and its people look like they are systemically racist. I have been all over this country and met with people of all colors and occupations. I have found the huge majority of Americans are good people who do not care about the color of a person's skin; they care about the content of a person's character, which is as it should be. We judge people by their actions, not their appearance. If someone flees the police, steals from neighbors, sells drugs, or pulls a gun on innocent people, that person does not have good character, regardless of race.

Homicide currently takes the lives of 3 percent of Black Americans; this is clearly not all from White police shooting Blacks or even Black police shooting Blacks. On the other hand, homicides barely register for White Americans. I know some will suggest socioeconomics as the sole cause of the disparity, but this is a faulty conclusion. We never solve problems for a child, a community, or an ethnicity by throwing money at the problems. Unfortunately, this is a liberal "solution" that has been posited for fifty years, and it backfires each time it is tried.

The War on Poverty was a program started by Democrats as a way to lift poor people—mostly minorities—out of poverty. Like so many well-meaning programs instituted at the expense of taxpayers, this one became a colossal failure. It started in 1964 as part of President Lyndon Johnson's State of the Union address and has since cost taxpayers tens of trillions of dollars (not including Social Security and Medicare). The bold attempt to erase poverty by government policy was doomed before it began. People are not motivated by handouts; the majority are motivated by opportunity. Most progressives think if you pay off student loans, give universal healthcare, or provide housing and food, people will be lifted up and out of poverty. This is exactly what President Johnson thought.

According to new studies, the War on Poverty failed completely. More of the population is less capable of self-sufficiency today than before the program began. Again, take a moment to think about that. This was a program designed to help Blacks and other minorities, but it had the opposite effect, creating intergenerational dependence on government and a financial burden to taxpayers. According to a report by the Heritage Foundation, "The unchanging poverty rate for the past 45 years is perplexing because anti-poverty or welfare spending during that period has simply exploded." Nearly 1 in 3 Americans receives benefits from one of eighty means-tested welfare programs. That's nearly $10,000 per recipient, and it still is not enough to effect the desired results. Don't take my word for it; read the studies for yourself. As the Heritage Foundation explained, the left uses "declining relative prices of many amenities to argue that even though poor households have air conditioning, computers, cable TV, and wide-screen TVs, they still suffer from substantial material deprivation in basic needs such as food and housing. Here again, the data tell a different story."[61]

While Johnson said he wanted to make "taxpayers out of tax-eaters," the opposite has happened. Transgenerational tax-eaters suck the life out of the economy and saddle hard-working Americans with further debt they neither wanted nor seem able to free themselves. One of the many factors in this generational dependency is that big government displaced fathers by giving them no incentive to stay and care for their offspring. In effect, government became what fathers had been before Johnson's well-meaning program. In the fifty years following the President's program, the unwed birthrate went from less than 5 percent to over 40 percent. The War on Poverty crippled marriage in low-income communities. The welfare state has also reduced self-sufficiency by providing economic rewards to able-bodied adults who do not work or who work comparatively little.[62]

"For the first time in our history it is possible to conquer poverty," said Johnson. Good intentions, no doubt, but this is how well-intentioned ideas go awry. We think the government is the solution to all our problems, and we become dependent on this amorphous entity to fix things. By making people dependent on subsidies, we do not lift them up; we keep them down. What went wrong with the War on Poverty? It treated poverty like a war to be won. We thought we could muster our willpower and defeat the enemy. Unfortunately, these programs did more to push Black Americans down than to lift them up. Liberals thought they owned Black votes because they kept creating this systemic dependency. Thankfully, the Black community has started to wake up to this form of liberal enslavement.

The bloodiest war America ever fought was against itself—the Civil War for the freeing of slaves and the emancipation of people. A whopping 620,000 war casualties amounted to one life lost for every six people freed. That is a big price. That is a price Republican President Abraham Lincoln willingly engaged. Why? Because he felt all people, regardless of color, deserved freedom. My friend, we have come a long way as a nation and as a people. We are not perfect, and we never will be. Does that mean we are a systemically racist country at the core? I do not believe we are, and my experience tells me this is a massive lie perpetuated by forces that intentionally want to keep us from unity, freedom, and interdependence.

The Lie of Systemic Racism

The Black Lives Matter website declares, "The enemy is now and has always been the four threats of white supremacy, patriarchy, capitalism, and militarism. These forces and not Islam create terrorism. These forces and not queerness create homophobia."

Anyone familiar with history knows this is nothing short of Marxist ideology masquerading as racial justice. Robin DiAngelo, author of *White Fragility* and a leading proponent of Critical Race Theory, said we need to create a culture that actually "spits out those who are resistant, as opposed to what it does now, which is to spit out those who want to break with White solidarity." She went on to say, "And I think people of color need to get away from White people and have some community with each other."[63] This form of deliberate segregation is a step backward in race relations. It fosters antipathy, draws wrong conclusions, and does extreme damage.

Taxpayers have been forking over tens of millions of dollars for Diversity, Equity, and Inclusion (DEI) education in the Pentagon. By executive order, the government directed all federal agencies to "establish or elevate Chief Diversity Officers." Kelisa Wing was one of these special agents selected to lead a DEI unit that involves curriculum and development in hiring. She is also the author of *What Is White Privilege?* She posted,

"I'm so exhausted as these white folx in these PD sessions this lady actually had the CAUdacity to say that black people can be racists too . . . . I had to stop the session and give Karen the BUSINESS."[64]

In Oklahoma, state representative Regina Goodwin declared, "DEI is a deity, diversity, equity, and inclusion is God."[65] There you have it, right out in the open. No apologies. We hear terms like microaggressions, equity, social justice, systemic racism, white privilege, intersectionality, implicit biases, non-binary, and more. What we need to know is that Critical Race Theory is divisive. It is destructive and based on false ideas and premises, something I don't have the time to unpack in this book. What I can say is that the four tenets include:

1. Racism is normal, permanent, and pervasive.
2. Racism is concealed beneath ideas like colorblindness, meritocracy, individualism, neutrality, and objectivity.
3. Lived experience is critical to understanding racism.
4. Racism is one of many interlocking systems of oppression including sexism, classism, and heterosexualism.

Perhaps you wonder, as I have, what the connection between LGBTQ, feminism, and racism is. Intersectionality explains it as authors Dr. Neil Shenvi and Dr. Pat Sawyer wrote in their book, *Critical Dilemma*: "CRT's commitment to the affirmation of homosexuality, same-sex marriage, and transgender is one of its 'defining elements.' To reject it is to reject one of CRT's defining elements."[66]

According to Critical Theorists, racism contributes to the very social fabric that makes America what it is today: income, imprisonment, health, housing, education, political representation, and military service. In other words, there is no fixing racism in the country because the entire structure that supports it must first be dismantled so it can be built back better. (Have you heard that phrase used somewhere before?) We are indebted to great thinkers like the late Robert Bork who, a quarter of a century ago, saw what was happening and tried to warn us. "Affirmative action is simply irrelevant to discrimination" he said. "Discrimination is alleged much more often than it exists . . . It is now fashionable to speak of seeking diversity, but the change in terms does not distinguish the fact of preference." And by preference, Bork was talking about preference to non-white minorities (except Asians). The real harm has led to greater antagonism and self-segregation, the kind espoused openly by Critical Theorists like Robin DiAngelo. This is unhelpful in every conceivable way to Blacks as well as Whites.

"One reason Afrocentrists are not challenged is that race is becoming a subject it is almost impossible to discuss honestly in public," wrote Bork.[67] He may have written that a quarter century ago, but we are there today. It is impossible to look at DEI as it pertains to professional sports—and not just basketball—and conclude there ought to be a greater representation of White players where Blacks predominate. In university admissions for science, Asians outperform Whites, and Whites outperform Blacks. The assumption that the discrepancies have to do with racial inequity is preposterous. It is well known that Asian students and their families have two defining characteristics: a culture that encourages education as a means of socioeconomic advancement, and intact families.

It is no secret that two-thirds of Black infants are born out of wedlock (18 percent for Whites). Marriage and family make a difference in educational attainment, vocational attainment, and generally keep young people out of trouble with law enforcement. Certainly, one of the solutions is to encourage fathers to stay and support their children, marry the children's mother, and offer a positive role-model for their offspring. To a large extent, this is not happening in Black communities, and the results speak for themselves. It is easy to blame White patriarchy or systemic racism rather than to look inside at what is broken. If disenfranchisement or racism were the sole factors keeping minority peoples down, why did Jews manage to rebuild their lives after suffering millions of deaths at the hands of the antisemitic Nazis? Surprisingly, 20 percent of all Nobel prizes have been awarded to Jews who make up a mere 1 percent of the world population. Is this because of White guilt or racism? If we use CRT logic—meaning that Blacks are kept from upward mobility because of lack of opportunity, prejudice, or systemic racism—wouldn't the same reasoning apply to Jews or Asian Americans? What we strive for in America is equality of opportunity, not equality of outcomes. Outcomes are based on personal decisions such as hard work, education, attitude, encouragement, and myriad other variables.

As Bork observed, "It is no wonder affirmative action creates hostilities . . . preferential policies do not build the incentives for individual development that are necessary to uplift a formerly oppressed people, or anybody else for that matter." The mistake we have made is to treat Blacks or Hispanics to varying standards, in some instances lowering standards for so-called victims of oppression. A recipe for disaster? You bet! And more than twenty-five years of experimentation has created systemic repression of White males. Proponents of CRT will argue this "leveling out" is necessary to rebalance the oppression of minorities, and I am not just talking about racial minorities.[68] The Supreme Court ruling against affirmative action by a 6-3 majority (along ideological lines) sent shock waves to liberal lawmakers who immediately called for "packing the Supreme Court." In other words, if you do not like a judicial decision, find a way to get what you want. What was the high court's sin? They struck down race-conscious admissions.

The Myth of Perfect Balance

My idea of fairness may be quite different than yours, and herein lies the problem of trying to balance ethnic division. We have come a long way in this country toward righting wrongs from our distant past, despite what we hear from the media. Racism and sexism have been ameliorated in the past fifty years and even earlier than that. Today, CRT and its supporters push us further apart rather than bring us closer together. This ideologically infused environment shuts down those who disagree, as we have seen on college campuses. A male has zero right to talk about abortion. He does not have a uterus, so he does not have the right to voice his opinion. White males are the oppressors of women and people of color; they are exploiters. If you or I think we have a right to speak, we will find out differently when we try speaking in a civil manner in a hostile environment.

Western culture is often seen as racist, sexist, violent, and imperialistic. None of this, of course, is based on reality, and that is precisely the point. If we feel oppressed, we must be, so our words must be accepted as truth. A person's "lived experience" supersedes dissent (the third tenant of Critical Theory). There is no transcendent truth; only subjective truth matters. And there lies the problem. When there is no objective benchmark for truth, everyone can determine their own truth based on their feelings. In today's world, feelings matter more than objective reality. Anyone who doubts this need only try explaining the science behind men not being able to give birth, the enormous health risks of homosexuality, or the fact that an unborn child is a human.

"Ignored reality transforms itself (reverts back) into the Goddess of Chaos," wrote Dr. Jordan Peterson. "Ignored reality manifests itself in an abyss of confusion and suffering."[69] Critical Race Theory, as well as Diversity, Equity, and Inclusion and the near limitless permutations of that sort of thinking, keep telling us that America is a bad place, police are bad, abortion is healthcare, a man can be a woman, and White men are the enemy of women and minorities. The purveyors of this divisive thinking fan the flames of division and tell people they are being persecuted, maligned, minimized, cheated, and discriminated against. There is only one major problem with this kind of rhetoric: it is false, a myth to deliberately foster chaos, an ignored reality. The reality is that Blacks are far better off today than they were fifty years ago. Women were far better off after the enactment of Title IX (though that is now in jeopardy because a handful of men want to compete against women in sports since they cannot win fairly against other men). In truth, there is a growing gender gap in higher education, both in enrollment and graduation rates. Young women are more likely to be enrolled in college today than young men; among those aged twenty-five and older, women are more likely than men to have a four-year college degree.[70] (Perhaps we should create a level-gender playing field for men in higher education, since more undergraduate and graduate degrees are conferred on women ...?)

My point is that if we are serious about equity, shouldn't we look at this trend and try to balance the number of males going to college by giving them special treatment or incentives, and in turn take incentives away from women? The idea of balancing everything in culture is not only a silly proposition, but also downright dangerous. When we try to force balance, someone always loses. For example, if equity in certain sports like basketball is applied, quotas should also be applied so more Whites could participate, which in turn would force out qualified Blacks. The same can be said for corporations that are forced or coerced into elevating more people of color. When you or I fly across country, do we check to see if the pilot is a woman, a Black man, or gay? Do we care? What difference does it make? If you are anything like me—and I hope in this case you are—don't you want the most qualified person flying the plane?

If we are watching our favorite sports team, do we care what color the players are? Of course not. We want the best players to represent our team. So why do we try to apply equity in academia, industry, politics, or any other corner of culture? Asians represent over 17 percent of the physicians in the U.S. but only 7 percent of the U.S. population. Should we balance this out and allow only a specific number of Asians to enter medical school so we can make room for other disenfranchised minority Americans? Do we want a surgeon operating on our heart who got into medical school with subpar grades and graduated because she received special treatment due to her ethnicity or sexual preferences? The fact is that a Black applicant is substantially more likely to be admitted to medical school than an Asian or White applicant with the same entry scores and GPA. If systemic injustice exists in medical school admissions, it certainly does not favor either Whites or Asians.

For a further study on this issue, I heartily encourage you to read *Critical Dilemma* by Shevni and Sawyer to gain a better understanding of the real existing imbalances and inequities and why they are escalating. The observations of Allan Bloom, long before the tidal wave of CRT invaded many institutions, made what may now be interpreted as racist though nothing he said was challenged as untrue. "Affirmative action now institutionalizes the worst aspects of separatism. The fact is that the average Black student's achievements do not equal those of the average White [or Asian] student in the good universities, and everybody knows it. It is also a fact that the university degree of a Black student is tainted, and employers look on it with suspicion or become guilty accomplices in the toleration of incompetence. The worst part of all this is that Black students, most who avidly support the system, hate its consequences. A disposition composed of equal parts of shame and resentment has settled on many Black students who are beneficiaries of preferential treatment."[71] Strong words by today's standards to be sure, but we have unwittingly—of course, all for the best of intentions—created further anxiety because we tried to create balance using the wrong methods. If Whites are to accept their communal guilt and shame, as some CRT theorists believe they should, the shame should be in using the wrong methods to try and "fix" a culture that can only be fixed by heart change. We do not fix tensions between Blacks and Whites, Asians and Hispanics by forcing one side to act in a way that will inevitably foster greater tension.

Which Way Up?

Let's end this chapter by quoting Martin Luther King. "Now there is a final reason I think that Jesus says, 'Love your enemies.' It is this: that love has within it a redemptive power. And there is a power there that eventually transforms individuals. Just keep being friendly to that person. Just keep loving them, and they can't stand it too long. Oh, they react in many ways in the beginning. They react with guilt feelings, and sometimes they'll hate you a little more at that transition period, but just keep loving them. And by the power of your love, they will break down under the load. That's love, you see. It is redemptive, and this is why Jesus says love. There's something about love that builds up and is creative. There is something about hate that tears down and is destructive. So love your enemies."[72]

This is a far different attitude than what we hear from Critical Race activists. Why? Because Dr. King sought to unite us as a people; CRT is a divisive philosophy that seeks to tear down. It seeks power, subjugation, control, and ultimate social upheaval. Jesus's goal was not to overthrow the government of Rome at the time; His purpose was to overthrow the darkness within the human heart. We can first take affirmative action and apply it to our own hearts. Only through internal transformation does external change occur. We cannot pass enough legislation to take away hate, bigotry, or antisemitism. We can never perfectly balance inequities. No matter how well meaning we are, trying to fix what's broken often creates the very inequities we wish to right. Instead, we continue to fumble along as a nation, seeking to do right, recognizing our imperfect history and encouraging people to be responsible citizens, caring for one another, and being responsible for our families and communities. To answer the question Rodney King asked at the press conference, "Yes, we can get along." We can choose a different life for ourselves and our families, one based on personal responsibility, respect for others, and hope for a better future.

CHAPTER SEVEN

The Depressing Reality: Why Young People Are Struggling

"Today in America the social order is fraying badly; we seem to be on a path of continuing social decline . . . People have become strong on individual rights and weak on community obligations."
—David Popenoe

The scene—and the reaction to it—was bizarre. Hundreds of teenagers and young adults descended on downtown Chicago, destroying cars, fighting in the streets, shooting guns, and creating havoc. What did then mayor-elect, Brandon Johnson, do? He cautioned against "demonizing" the vandals. "It is not constructive to demonize youth who have otherwise been starved of opportunities in their own communities." This same mayor has come under fire for comments made in support of "defunding the police" and trying to reallocate money for social spending and therapeutic approaches. Starved for opportunities? Therapeutic approaches? What exactly does this mean?

Liberalism, for all its seemingly good intentions, does not work anymore than did the rehabilitation model of the '60s and '70s. I am certainly not against programs like the YMCA that keep kids in sports or other healthy activities. These diversionary programs can be helpful to some youth. But kids who smash car windows, spray paint businesses, fight in the streets, and shoot guns are engaging in criminal activity. It is not demonizing them to call them criminals. When we care more about stigmatization than we do illegal conduct, something is backward. Disturbing trends in American youth today are real and cannot be easily dismissed as "demonizing teens and youth." Serious problems do not simply disappear by relabeling or ignoring them.

Studies show that nearly half of all teens are depressed, feeling persistent sadness and hopelessness. Some take drugs or drink alcohol in an attempt to kill the pain. And tragically, these young people are committing suicide at unprecedented rates. What do young adults have to be so depressed about? Look at the headlines. Melting glaciers, toxic waste, imminent war, widespread drought, Fentanyl poisoning, government gridlock, rioting in the streets, and an increasingly shaky economy. Kids growing up today might easily wonder what they have to look forward to. After the widespread fear and disillusionment during the pandemic, is it any wonder kids struggle emotionally? Was it helpful to isolate a segment of the population who had next to zero chance of dying from COVID?

Drugs have become the choice of many youths seeking to escape the realities of real or imagined catastrophes. According to the National Center for Drug Abuse Statistics, drug use went up 61 percent among eighth-graders in a five-year span. Meanwhile, nearly two out of three high schoolers have abused alcohol. Where, you might wonder, are the parents? We will address this a bit later in the chapter. Meanwhile, here is a snapshot of what is happening in America today.

- 4,777 Americans aged fifteen to twenty-four died from overdosing on illicit drugs in a single year (well ahead of firearm deaths, though mainstream media will tell you otherwise).
- 62 percent of teens have abused alcohol by grade 12.
- Nearly half a million youth aged twelve to seventeen meet the criteria for Alcohol Use Disorder.
- Since 1999, overdose deaths due to opioids have increased 500 percent among fifteen- to twenty-four-years olds.
- U.S. Customs and Border Protection seizure figures show that 99.8 percent of methamphetamine and 99.9 percent of marijuana seized in the U.S. came from the southern border.[73]
- More than 70,000 people died of overdose from synthetic opioids in 2021, according to the CDC—a number representing two out of three of all fatal drug overdoses and more lives lost than the combined equivalent of U.S. military personnel killed during the wars in Vietnam, Iraq, and Afghanistan.[74]

Mental health problems, like depression or suicidal ideation, are directly associated with increased drug use. Taking drugs is often associated with a sense of despair, yet despite the massive seizures of drugs along our southern border, some politicians want open borders. While border policy is not our focus here, the inescapable truth is that American citizens are at risk because we refuse to take border security seriously. If our police, our children, and our communities are less safe because of open borders, there surely must be a reason progressives want them to remain open. These progressives can scream and holler all they want about school shootings or limiting assault weapons, but no one will take this conversation seriously unless the left decides the 70,000 people dying each year from opioids are equally as valuable as those killed or injured in school shootings.

Prophets of Doom

I find it strangely ironic that we have pushed self-esteem on youth for the past twenty years, but on issues like global warming, the COVID pandemic, the economy, or even faith, the left has managed to foster gloom and doom in our teens. In fact, I would say the left consistently fosters negativity and hopelessness, which does not help adults, and it certainly does not help young people.

We have force-fed our children bogus self-esteem by conferring trophies, participation medals, and ribbons on them, just for showing up—in sports, at work, or at school. Being rewarded for showing up is simply not good enough. Certainly, we have to be there to participate, but achievement counts for something, as it should. We have gone from this lopsided esteem nonsense to our unwillingness to see anything good in the world. If we have no hope for the future, why put in the effort at school or work? Many youths today have developed a somewhat fatalistic view of the world, which is unhelpful to them and to our communities. But why are we surprised by this?

Former Vice President Spiro Agnew once referred to politicians as "nattering nabobs of negativism." Negativity is psychologically demoralizing. Negative people simply cannot stop talking about how the sky is falling, much like Henny-Penny in the Chicken Little story, which goes something like this: One morning, as Henny-Penny was plucking worms in the henyard, an acorn dropped from a tree right onto her head. She had no idea what had hit her, however, and so she started shouting, "The sky is falling! The sky is falling!" She ran around in circles for a while, calmed herself, and then got right to waddling—she had to alert the king!

We see how fear, negativity, and hopelessness motivated Henny-Penny. If we are not careful, they can motivate us as well—and even begin to rule our lives if we let them.

Metaphorically speaking, we will all have acorns drop on our heads at some point in life. Life is tough. Life is not always fair. Those of us who have lived long enough know that bad things happen, sometimes dropping in on us like unwelcome acorns. Then what? We can panic and create panic for others by drawing false conclusions, or we can accept our realities and move on the best we can. People who live in a state of perpetual victimhood, however, do not move on. Instead, they bask in their plight, whatever they think it is. They rarely improve their condition and blame everything and everyone for their failures . . . except themselves.

The blame is everywhere today. It is like a cancer destroying us from the inside out. Personal responsibility, not blame, is how we find success in life and in relationships. As Jordan Peterson put it, "The idea of a value-free choice is a contradiction in terms. Value judgements are a precondition for action. Furthermore, every activity, once chosen, comes with its own internal standard of accomplishment . . . If there was no better or worse, nothing would be worth doing. There would be no value, and therefore, no meaning."[75] Discovering meaning in life is what many young people struggle to find in our increasingly complex and divisive world. While we listen to globalists decry the impact of fossil fuels on the future of the earth, we see them jump into their private jets for some important meeting in Davos, Park City, or some other exotic destination. Perhaps the ends justify the means for some elitists, but the rest of us are relegated to higher gas prices, electric vehicles (which we cannot afford), and being forced to give up our gas stoves and lawn mowers. The elites use doomsday clocks, doomsday sea rises, doomsday nuclear war, and doomsday pandemics to control and manipulate the masses. Sadly, most of the time, they are successful. But the side effects are distraught, depressed, and suicidal youth. This hardly seems a fair tradeoff, does it?

"Ideologues are people who pretend they know how to 'make the world a better place' before they've taken care of their chaos within," Dr. Peterson declared.[76] I have come to the conclusion these ideologues really do believe in their mission, but belief and right action are not the same. We must remain intractable for right belief before we engage in what we think is right action. Again, this is where our worldviews matter; if our worldview does not leave room for God, for a better tomorrow, for a hope-filled future, we are in serious trouble.

Jesus said, "The thief comes only to steal and kill and destroy; I have come that they may have life, and have it to the full" (John 10:10). Christianity is about hope, about a good future, and about changed lives. From my vantage point, it is Christ, not drag shows, surgical removal of one's genitals, or revolution, that brings ultimate hope. The gospel is called "The Good News" for a reason. No matter what happens in our lives or in the world, we still have hope. This is the message we need to tell our kids, our grandkids, our friends, and our neighbors. The world is not as bad as we are told; the sky is not falling. This does not mean there are no problems to face. We will always have problems—in our personal lives and in the world. But we can help the next generation by giving them hope, as well as the tools they need to succeed. As I said earlier, sometimes the remedies for what ails us are not the solutions we are willing to accept. Instead, we look everywhere except to the obvious. The reason we do this is because change is something that must happen inside of us instead of "out there somewhere." For that reason, we often resist change, even when we suspect it might be for the better.

Fatherless Homes

Let's start with one of the most obvious and universal factors for building positivity and a strong worldview into our children: fathers. Fathers matter to kids. When divorce rates began to skyrocket and children were separated from their fathers, they began to suffer in ways sociologists never anticipated. The impact since has been a significant cost to society. Homes where the father is absent suffer numerous negative impacts from higher rates of incarceration, precocious sexuality, drug and alcohol use and abuse, lower academic performance, school drop-out rates, and pregnancy. For single moms raising children (and this accounts for about 86 percent of post-divorce homes), the situation gets worse as upward socioeconomic mobility is stifled. This leads to poverty and translates to higher government (taxpayer) subsidies.

The stigma that used to accompany divorce no longer exists. Divorce is easy despite the impact on children. So what do kids of divorce have to say? That was a question researcher Judith Wallerstein asked, and here are some of her results. "Children of divorce also share a morality, one that is even more conservative than their parents. As a group, they want what their parents did not achieve—a good marriage, commitment, romantic love that lasts, and faithfulness. The word *faithful* comes up again and again in our interviews."[77]

Ironically, young people think they can avoid their parents' mistakes or poor decisions by living together before getting married. Sadly, statistics show the opposite, with a direct correlation between living together before marriage and a higher incidence of divorce. This may seem counter-intuitive in today's world; as a result, it does not seem to deter the mythology. People still set up house before tying the knot, but this only complicates things financially and emotionally. "The children of divorce," wrote Wallerstein, "have an old-fashioned view of the rules of marriage. They are disdainful of concepts of serial monogamy and open marriage, and compared with their parents they are a morally conservative group. The return to more traditional values, however, is not rooted in theology but stems from their own gut-wrenching unhappiness over the experience of divorce."[78]

These observations are not intended to heap guilt on those who have been through divorce, as millions have, but rather to bring a clear perspective about unintended impacts. We have heard divorce rationalized with arguments such as "children are quite resilient" and "parents need to be true to themselves." These excuses only assuage the decision-makers—the adults, never the children. Most kids clearly want nothing more than for their parents to stay together. A divorce is the severing of continuity, however imperfect the union may be. Divorce is the death of a mini society. Mothers *and* fathers are essential to the good of children and to society. As David Popenoe wrote, "Few people have doubts about the fundamental importance of mothers. But fathers? More and more the question is being raised, are fathers necessary?" He goes on to observe, "Across time and cultures, fathers have always been essential—and not just for their sperm. Indeed, until today, no known society ever thought of fathers as unnecessary."[79]

In the Black community, more than seven in ten children grow up without a father in the home. This is not about racism; this is about values. Where do these kids learn to relate to authority if not in the home? Fatherhood is not some "patriarchal invention" forced on society. Fathers who left their home or children used to be called "deadbeat dads" or "deviants."

This is no longer the case, and perhaps that is unfortunate. Fathers play a critical role in steering boys toward healthier ideas about masculinity. Ironically, young men tend to be more traditional in how they express their masculinity. They tend to take on the same view of masculinity as their fathers—if one is present in the home. This suggests boys learn what it means to be a man from their father; they emulate them and adopt similar values and ideas. Boys raised in single-parent, female-headed homes have a distinct disadvantage regarding what it means to be a man.

In his book *Iron John*, Robert Bly wrote about the transition to manhood. "It's becoming clear to us that manhood doesn't happen by itself; it doesn't just happen because we eat Wheaties. The active intervention of older men welcomes the younger man into the ancient mythologized, instinctive male world." [80] But it is more than lack of a male rite of passage that keeps boys from becoming men. Often in a female-headed home, a mom will deliberately or inadvertently prevent the transition. By focusing on keeping their sons safe—to protect them from the big mean world—mothers will not allow their sons to be brave, take risks, push themselves dangerously, or have the freedom to engage in adventurous pursuits. While protecting a boy is what mothers instinctively do, pushing their sons to take risks is what fathers do. In the absence of a father, how are boys to learn that?

It is of little surprise to me that in recent years boys have become weaker, both physically and emotionally. The advent of males dressing up as females may well be part of a grown man's way of becoming his mother—not literally of course, but at least in a figurative sense. A boy who cannot make it in a man's world may reject his masculine self. He may look for the acceptance he does not have in a father and seek it out in other males, hoping gay men will accept him rather than just use him for their own needs. Some boys act out in violence. This may be from an overcompensated understanding of what real men do—or because they are pushing back against an over-feminized and over-protected boyhood. I do not say this as an indictment against women and mothers, but rather against a culture where fathers are absent in the lives of boys—often because they are told their masculinity is toxic, misplaced, unwanted, or harmful. These messages have sent many men into a form of retreat. They find themselves in an emotional cul-de-sac with no place to turn around. In my experience, most women are not attracted to weak men. To the contrary, women are drawn to the strength and protection of men. There are, of course, some women who prefer to dominate men or coddle their sons. This inevitably leads to passive men and weak sons who misunderstand what healthy masculinity looks like.

Bly wrote, "During the last thirty years men have been asked to learn how to go with the flow, how to follow rather than lead, how to live in a non-hierarchal way, how to be more vulnerable, how to adopt consensus decision-making. Some women want a passive man if they want a man at all . . . Passivity increases as the educational system turns out 'products.'"[81] Today we watch as young men exorcise their demons, their frustrations, their misunderstanding of police, or capitalism, or some injustice they feel entitled to fix with violence against the very institutions that give them a chance to protest. The weakness is generation-wide. A study of Gen-Zers (young men and boys born after 1997), found they lack communication skills, effort, motivation, and even technological skills. Gen-Zers are being canned from their jobs because they are "too easily offended." According to 75 percent of managers and business leaders, they are more difficult to work with than other generations. Working with them, managers say, can be exhausting because they lack discipline and have difficulty taking orders without arguing. [82]

What about teen girls? A Center for Disease Control and Report show almost 60 percent of U.S. girls reported persistent sadness and hopelessness; almost no one seems to have a good answer for this. Some people point their finger at bullying, social media, sexual threats, body image, or friendship struggles. I do not doubt these may contribute to the sadness some girls feel, but what about home life? What about divorce and/ or a father's absence? For most analysts, these factors scarcely register on the radar of explanations. Again, many people do not really want the cure. And there is a good reason why they do not, but we will talk about this in a moment.

Do you really believe girls have it worse today than in any previous generations? Sure, we can acknowledge there is widespread pressure to do well in school or to look like the latest supermodel. If girls are depressed because they do not have the newest iPhone, best figure, or more "likes" on social media, then these are first-world issues. I am not going to say these issues are not real, but I am going to say they demonstrate something much deeper—that girls lack coping skills to deal with real-world issues. Like boys, girls are growing up emotionally weaker than previous generations. The long-term effects for both sexes are troubling. They lack the skills that enable them to cope with everyday issues, and these skills come primarily from fathers. In their book, *Raising Boys by Design*, Dr. Gregory Jantz and Michael Gurian list what fathers bring to the lives of their sons and daughters.

- Bond with children in shorter bursts of contact
- Teach order, pattern thinking, ritualized action
- Downplay emotional, play up performance
- Promote risk-taking and independence
- Increase strength in child response by decreasing vulnerability
- Promote hierarchal deference to authority if the authority figure is respectable
- Encourage action as a primary path to self-worth
- Help children feel strong, not necessarily better[83]

What can we learn from these studies and statistics? First, we must acknowledge the vital impact fathers have on their children. Second, we need to stop blaming everything except the breakdown of the nuclear family for making our children weaker. Third, we can determine to protect and nurture our children in positive, life-affirming ways rather than coddling them. Fourth, we can keep our marriages strong and continue to fight against the temptation to leave when the going gets tough.

We have watched as widespread individualism has ruined the lives of millions of children. This is a philosophy that says, "My needs come first." This concept is expressed in many ways, but essentially it elevates SELF above children, above conjugal commitment, and above society. Being true to oneself supplants being true to kids and fails to recognize the larger impacts on

society. We are big on talking about self-reliance, self-sufficiency, self-improvement, or self-development, but weak on
putting our own wants or needs aside long enough to think past
ourselves and make the necessary sacrifices for others.

The remedy to our broken children may start with the
"N-word," the word few parents dare to use these days. This
simple but powerful two-letter word is well within the grasp of
parents, but they often refuse to use it even when it is needed
most. As you have no doubt figured out by now, the word is
"NO." How many times have we heard parents say they cannot
take a particular game away from their son or a phone from
their daughter? They struggle to say no even to keep them from
going to wild parties or having sex. My question is this: Whose
house do they live in? Who pays the bills? Who is responsible for helping them make good decisions? Kids have become
weaker because they have far more privileges than they have
responsibilities. Would it surprise you to know that kids crave
boundaries? Probably not. Kids without boundaries are often
kids who do not feel loved. They do not just want or need mate-
rial objects; they want and need quality time. And quality time
is the one thing many parents are not willing to make room for
in their busy lives.

Like it or not, children thrive in a traditional two-parent
household. Most flourish with clear expectations and structure.
Forty years ago, a group of psychologists decided that having
fences around schools inhibited children. The kids needed a
sense of freedom, they argued. By removing the fences, kids
would no longer feel they were in a prison camp. The psychologists had the chain-link fences taken down around one school

to see how the kids would respond. When the fences were in place, the children inside the school grounds often wandered near the fences but not beyond them. When the fences were removed, the children moved toward the center of the school-yard because they no longer felt safe. They actually felt safer knowing there were fences in place. And it is not just physical safety they crave, though this is important too.

I am not so naive as to believe our children will not complain about the fences we establish in their lives. Let them. We simply remind them why we establish rules (fences) in our home—to protect them. Consistency and continuity in a child's life—such as routines, expectations, and boundaries—all speak of parental love, not the opposite. In his final words on earth, Moses spoke to the Jewish people and said, "Take to heart all the words I have solemnly declared to you this day, so that you may command your children to obey carefully all the words of this law. They are not just idle words for you—*they are your life*" (Deuteronomy 32:46-47, emphasis added). What were these "words of the law," and why were they so important? They were the Creator's way of giving His people strong, healthy boundaries in life and relationships. We can do the same.

A Final Word

Former Secretary of Education William Bennett made these observations in his book *The Moral Compass.* "There are many obligations in life, but none more important than the ones we accept when we become husbands and wives, mothers and fathers . . . In recent history, marriage has devolved from being a sacrament to a contract to a convention, to finally, a convenience." He went on to observe, "For most of us, the obligations of parenthood eventually go hand in hand with those of marriage. No duty is more important than the nurture and protection of children, and if parents do not teach honesty, perseverance, self-discipline, a desire for excellence, and a host of basic skills, it is exceedingly difficult for any of society's institutions to teach those things in the parent's place."[84]

There are plenty of people in our society who will gladly teach our children. In fact, some believe parents should butt out of teaching and educating their own children and leave the indoctrination to the "professionals." Our job as parents is not to abnegate our responsibility to model and teach godly values to our children. If not us, who? If not us, how can we expect them to absorb values that will make them good citizens? Millions of children are hurting today. They are confused, hopeless, disillusioned, and self-medicating. Negativity breeds hopelessness. Hopelessness fosters depression. Depression leads to substance abuse. Substance abuse leads to suicide. Our children need hope, encouragement, boundaries. We can give these things to them. We *must* give these things to them. And we can give them something else—stability in our marriages and consistency in our values.

CHAPTER EIGHT

Educating Ourselves to Ignorance

"We have no government armed with power capable of contending with human passions unbridled by morality and religion. Our constitution was made only for a moral and a religious people. It is wholly inadequate for a government of any other."
—John Adams

Ian Haworth, a writer and podcast host, had been invited to speak by the UAlbany chapter of Turning Point USA, a conservative group. The students shouted against him and chanted for an hour. Social media posts and posters read, "Drown out transphobia." What was Haworth's unpardonable sin? He "believes in biology and opposes genital mutilation being carried out on children." If this does not sound worthy of protest, you would be drawing the right conclusion. University students who are supposed to learn chemistry, biology, and open-minded debate know little of this in today's rapidly disintegrating campus environment. These same students responded by filling the meeting room at Assembly Hall and chanting epithets including "F__ you, TPUSA!" and "Ian sucks!" At one point, they formed an improvised conga line and called for Haworth to come out. When Avery Middendorf, the president of TPUSA at UAlbany, tried to speak, they drowned him out by shouting, "We can't hear you!"

"This type of protest is becoming much more common," said Zach Greenberg, senior program officer at the Foundation for Individual Rights and Expression, based in Philadelphia. "Students have gone from holding signs, debating, questioning (their opponents)—really debating the issues—to shouting them down," he said. "I think it really just shows a lack of knowledge about a free-speech culture . . . You do not have the right to drown out someone else." Protesters acknowledged their express intent was to shut Haworth down and then use the resulting attention to highlight what they see as threats to the transgender community.[85]

This sort of disruption is happening on college campuses across the country, and it's happening for an express purpose: to stomp out reason and dissent. Campuses, the very institutions once considered a forum for free expression, are now in lockstep with fascism, which is a tendency toward or actual exercise of strong autocratic or dictatorial control. Once upon a time, just a few decades ago, there was no enemy other than the man who was not open to hearing everything. How education has changed! Now people cannot express beliefs that run against any number of ideologies that permeate so-called higher education. "The gradual stifling of the old political and religious echoes in the souls of the young accounts for the difference between the students that I knew at the beginning of my teaching career and those I now face," said Professor Alan Bloom.[86]

Corruption at the Top

Randi Weingarten, head of the American Federation of Teachers, is so extremist in her views it comes as little surprise that our schools are in trouble with her as the head. She thinks banning Critical Race Theory is tantamount to racism. She thinks if parents don't want their children indoctrinated by drag queens, perverse books, or gay clubs, they must be homophobic. She's an outspoken, anti-conservative, anti-Christian, hate-filled pro-abortionist. "We're not indoctrinating," she said. "We're not grooming . . . What we're doing is making sure we educate kids."[87] She believes conservatives are bullies because they don't want their children taught what the parents consider lies about history, science, race, or faith. She believes conservatives who show up at schoolboard meetings to express their concern over what their children are being taught should shut up and let teachers do their jobs. She thinks we are brainwashing our own children by taking them to church, sharing time-tested moral values, and protecting them from filth and smut. Do you know what I think? I think good parents are tired of hearing about leftist educators who disparage this great nation, trash our cherished values, rewrite our history, treat police as if they were enemies, and advocate for unhealthy lifestyles.

Weingarten's definition of educating kids has everything to do with indoctrination. If this were not so, why is the U.S. falling so far behind the rest of the world in education? According to Business Insider, we are twenty-seventh in the world when it comes to our children's education.[88] (We were sixth in 1990.) Let that sink in for a moment!

While Weingarten talks about improving education, she and her ilk have quite obviously taken us in the opposite direction. Why the huge fall? It is at least partially due to pushing everything from DEI (Diversity, Equity, and Inclusion), CRT (Critical Race Theory), and LGBTQ+ instead of teaching core subjects. Some of the insane degrees college graduates now have—which taxpayers are supposed to subsidize—include gender studies, ethical hacking, puppetry, cannabis cultivation, surf studies, bagpiping, sexual studies, pop culture, comedy, and bowling management to name a few. What we hear from the liberal elites is that we are not spending enough on education. According to them, we would see better results if we put more money toward education—which they insist is for the future of our children. Throwing money at any problem seems to be the first and easiest answer for those who refuse to look at deeper issues. But is this a valid argument? Would more money really solve the problem? Here is the truth: the United States spends more money on education than any other country, but students still lag behind academically.[89] We spend $700 billion a year on education to rank twenty-seventh in the world. We are twenty-fourth in science and thirty-eighth in math. But I imagine students excel at learning all that is wrong with the police and all that is good about discovering their sexual proclivities.

If you think Weingarten is embarrassed by all this, you are wrong. Instead of being open to fairness—a basic value we hope our students learn in school—she believes it is the duty of higher education to discriminate against certain groups. For instance, she believes racial preferences help offset the inequities, created by teachers' unions, in K-12 education. High-achieving Asian-American and White students must be discriminated against to make up for the educational "privileges" that unions deny to minorities.[90]

Does this seem like a fair system to you? Does discriminating against Whites or Asians make sense? Imagine if you were in the situation where Jon Wang found himself. An eighteen-year-old student with a 4.65 high-school GPA and a perfect score on the SAT's math section was rejected by MIT, CalTech, Princeton, Harvard, Carnegie Mellon, and the University of California Berkeley. "I gave them my test scores, and then they must've run the model on that . . . [they] told me I had a 20% chance of getting accepted to Harvard as an Asian American and a 95% chance as an African American."[91] This is where affirmative action has failed everybody, not just Asians or Whites. It is exactly why in 2023 the Supreme Court wisely ruled against this form of discrimination.

Former Secretary of State Mike Pompeo put this educational catastrophe in perspective. His extensive experience led him to fire a shot into the culture war that may have struck a nerve when he offered his take on who is "the most dangerous person in the world." The former government official's career took him from a captain in the U.S. Army to the House of Representatives, CIA director, and then head of the State Department.

When he expressed that America's biggest threat is not from a foreign power but from a teacher's union, a lot of people gasped in disbelief. "I tell the story often. I get asked 'Who's the most dangerous person in the world?' The most dangerous person in the world is Randi Weingarten."[92]

I do not disagree with Pompeo, but I would add something else. Weingarten is grossly incompetent. She has failed America's schools; she has failed America's children. And she's failed parents she considers the enemy—the hard-working people who pay taxes to keep public schools running and who expect more from public education than leftist indoctrination and ridicule of parents' beliefs. This kind of education is clearly not what has made America great; it is just the opposite. This mentality—the haughty, self-righteous attitude of leftists who have been draining money, draining hope, and weakening our educational system—is the problem. I encourage you to attend schoolboard meetings, run for office, ask questions, find out what is happening in your district. This is a good place to start.

Christian values are not the only ones at stake here. Jews are facing discrimination too, particularly as anti-Semitism spans the globe. According to acclaimed attorney Alan Dershowitz, Zionist and conservative students are terrified to express their views on campus. "If you're, for example, an Orthodox Jew at a major institution today and wear a kippah or Star of David and you are perceived as being a Zionist, you're no longer allowed to join clubs, speak at clubs. At Berkley, for example, 14 clubs—and this is the University of California Law School." Dershowitz says he can no longer speak at any of those clubs about abortion, gay rights, or the powers of the Constitution. He has been banned.[93] This is precisely what happened in Nazi Germany as Hitler ascended to power—silencing opposition, bullying, thuggery, and ultimately execution. Have we learned nothing from history? Today's higher education has created "uni-thinkers," people offended by any idea that fails to coincide with their own. If this is not the result of indoctrination, what is it? Dershowitz observed, "We are now seeing an abolition of grades of meritocracy and the introduction of propaganda. Instead of teaching students how to think, teachers are insisting on teaching them *what to think* and not brooking any dissent and letting it be reflected in grades."[94]

Follow the Money

You would think educating the nation's children would be a bipartisan effort. We want our kids to succeed; we want our nation to succeed. We want our children to feel safe and protected while in school. We want to compete effectively with other nations in industry and commerce. Education is a form of intellectual property. We protect this because we know our vested interests and even our future are at stake. But this is wishful thinking. Though teachers' unions give verbal allegiance to kids, they have proven to be more interested in pushing their political agenda.

According to one report, the unions buy political influence outright. The National Education Association and the American Federation of Teachers—the nation's two biggest teachers' unions—are among the largest donors to politicians, and at least 94 percent of that money goes to Democrats. The laws in thirty-eight states guarantee collective bargaining, not just over pay but often over every aspect of the school day, even curriculum. Unions block school reform, oppose standardized testing, merit pay, and teacher accountability. They load the curriculum with political indoctrination—what they refer to as "social justice."[95]

For anyone wondering how schools have become so liberal, this is how it happened—union dues spent on indoctrination rather than education. These massive unions have millions of dollars to use on influence pedaling, and nearly all that money finds its way into the hands of Democrats and left-leaning politicians. There is simply no accountability. However, in deep-red states, people are waking up to what has been happening. As a result, they are banning unions from deducting dues from teachers' paychecks—money often used for purposes that weaken school districts and go against parental values. This needs to stop. This form of extortion by liberal school unions plays a major role in the indoctrination process Randi Weingarten claims is not happening. But there is more.

Changing Boundaries

Here is another reason our children are falling hopelessly behind. As we know, massive school districts in New York, Illinois, and California placed children in lockdowns during the pandemic. As a result, grades plummeted, participation waned, and depression increased. The segment of the population least likely to die from the exploited pandemic were systematically kept home from school, and the unions were the first to jump on this bandwagon. The already dreadful math and reading scores fell even further. In New York, some clever board-of-education bureaucrats came up with an idea to test these kids after the pandemic and see how they would score. As should have been expected, the abysmally low scores soon became the new normal. These board-of-education bureaucrats then defined proficiency downward—to the lowest possible numbers. How does this help children excel? Again, to anyone looking on, the answer is obvious: it does not. Defining proficiency downward celebrates mediocrity and creates an illusion by making students think they are doing better than they really are.

Barbara is a public-school educator who has taught high school English for twenty years. When I asked how her students fared after returning to the classroom, she said, "It has been an absolute disaster. You can't expect students who are at home while their parents work to spend hours a day doing studies. It just wasn't realistic. It didn't work." Although conscientious and caring about all her pupils, Barbara admitted that students with solid work-and-study ethics continued to learn, while those without classroom discipline fell further behind.

This brings us to another issue that has systematically weakened American education, even if union representatives refuse to acknowledge it. We simply cannot improve performance—in school, at work, or in government—by downgrading standards. This should be self-evident, but apparently it is not. Industry standards exist for a reason. For instance, building standards protect consumers from shoddy builders. Over time, we learn how to accommodate the standards rather than look for ways to weaken those standards. We have rules in sports, too. Imagine what would happen if a major-league umpire decided to change the distance between the pitcher's mound and home plate or change the strike zone for some players but not for others. Perhaps it would be fairer if we changed the strike zone to include anything within a foot of the plate to give pitchers with poor control a better opportunity to throw strikes. Ludicrous, you say, and you would be right— yet it lines up with the idea that downgrading standards helps our children.

We never elevate children by lowering standards. We lift them up by encouraging them to attain higher standards. For decades, we have worried more about self-esteem than about performance. A child's positive performance serves to bolster his self-esteem, not the other way around. Success is a process, not a one-time effort. So what about children who grow up in a drug-infested ghetto? Don't they deserve a chance to excel? Of course, they do. Is it easy? Absolutely not. But in modern-day America, opportunities for even the most disadvantaged children are clearly available to those who sacrifice, persevere, and work to improve themselves. Instead, nearly all we hear today is a litany of disadvantages and how we should right them, generally by throwing more taxpayer money at the problem. Children excel when we eliminate their excuses for non-performance and hold them accountable for their own future. To the left-leaning unionists, this sounds unkind and harsh. They prefer to keep less advantaged students in a state of victimhood. If a child *feels* he is a victim of an unfair system, how does this offer any motivation to get out of his situation?

With American students so far behind other countries in academic attainment, changing the boundaries by making that attainment easier is no solution. We do our children a great disservice by telling them, "Despite your poor performance, you are really smart enough, so we will give you a C grade instead of fail you." As my friend and teacher Barbara told me, most students in her rural district simply stopped doing their work when they were kept home from school. "You can't force kids to study. You can't make kids want to succeed. All you can do is give them encouragement and opportunity. The rest is up to them."

Indoctrination or Education?

At Edison High School in mostly conservative Huntington Beach, California, math students were forced by the female teacher to watch a gay-pride video. One of the students filmed this incident. While watching this film of students being force-fed gay-pride indoctrination, students are heard reacting negatively to what they are seeing, even groaning loudly and calling out "stop" and "turn it off" as the teacher plays the "Pride Month" video. One student even shouted, "Why are you showing this to kids?" In response, the teacher scolded the students and warned them they would have to watch it in Saturday school if they continued to make noise.

Let me ask two obvious questions. First, what does a gay-pride video have to do with learning math? With American students already way behind other nations in math proficiency, how does such a video help improve math scores? Second, when the teacher threatens students for being "inappropriate" because they oppose the video in the classroom, who is actually inappropriate here—the students or the teacher? Dissent being labeled inappropriate is the first indication that free speech and moral values are being stifled. This is what we call indoctrination or silence opposition. Shame the students, and threaten them with punishment.

A local LGBTQ supporter, upset about the students' reaction, shared the full video on social media. Did the person who shared that video think people of faith, people with values, people who care about their children should applaud and embrace those indoctrination efforts? We do not, and we will not. This kind of proselytizing has no place in public schools. As much as this fact may cause the gay community consternation, they must realize they will never have full acceptance for their lifestyle among those who see it as unhealthy and aberrant. No matter how much they try to infiltrate schools, churches, or businesses, most Americans are weary of the pressure. These doctrines have no place in schools. Period.

The video starts with a rainbow flag flying in the wind and the words "Pride Month" highlighted on the screen. Two women are shown embracing with noses touching, as other images of LGBTQ couples play on screen. "Don't forget to love each other," the video message says as it ends. No matter how hard people try to sanitize, normalize, standardize, or legitimatize homosexuality, our children do not need to be subjected to this message in their schools. But this is not the only message that is being crammed down their throats.

One headline reads, "DEI programs in universities are being cut across the country. What does this mean for higher education?"[96] Remember, DEI stands for Diversity, Equity, and Inclusion. The headline sounds like cutting DEI programs are tantamount to going back to the Dark Ages. As I mentioned in the previous example, students are inundated with non-academic nonsense ad nauseum. Rather than harming the children's education, cutting these reckless and unnecessary programs might very well enable students to concentrate on core subjects for a change.

More than a dozen state legislatures have introduced or passed bills reining in DEI programs in colleges and universities, claiming the programs eat up valuable financial resources with little impact. Of course, they do. Who needs more chief diversity officers? Do we really need someone telling students they are privileged or they must watch mandatory videos that push incipient racism? The diversity programs can include anything from reproductive rights (another term for pro-abortion rights) to White privilege, indigenous rights, reparations, and even global warming. None of this, I would add, belongs in education. This is especially true when we watch so-called progressives singlehandedly take us from a world powerhouse in education just thirty-five years ago to a dreadful ranking today. The left talks a good talk—"children first, children are our future"—but if these statements were true, we would see better results. If we allow educators to indoctrinate our children into ignorance, America will fall ever farther behind the rest of the world or continue to import intellectual property from countries that care more about math and science than they do LGBTQ rights or DEI.

The Role of Parents in Education

You may be surprised to learn that every collegiate institution founded in the colonies before the Revolutionary War was started by Christians—the lone exception is the University of Pennsylvania. This includes Harvard, Yale, Princeton, Rutgers, Rhode Island, Dartmouth, Northwestern, Columbia, Brown—all Christian. The Catholics started their universities too—Notre Dame, University of San Diego, Xavier, St, Mary's, Loyola Marymount, Boston College, Villanova, and others. The Jesuits and Mormons also have their own, like Gonzaga and BYU.

Can you think of even one university started by atheists? Neither can I. For decades now, Christians in this country have been seen as backward, out of touch with science, buffoons, or just plain ignorant. Much of this misplaced bias came from the so-called Enlightenment, the idea than man can perfect himself. Proponents of this type of thinking believe we can, as Thomas Jefferson maintained, continue to progress to the point where we are responsible for our own morality, without the benefit of intrusive, restrictive, or narrow-minded religion. Jefferson was a Unitarian who believed not only in the perfectibility of man but in the superiority of science to solve any problem mankind faced. People of faith have never been anti-science. Instead, we believe science comes from a Creator, and all we see in the world around us is not by accident. It is, in fact, by design. Christians believe the world is not random. We believe it was established for a purpose and can be understood using science. Many early scientists were also devout Christians; because they wanted to know more about God, they became scientists to learn more about the universe He created.

Humanism, a byproduct of Enlightenment thinking, dismisses the uniqueness of man and places faith in an inferior category, with no place for miracles. Adherents to this ideology believe everything can be explained through the scientific method. But as Professor Allan Bloom noted, "Cultural relativism [a byproduct of the Enlightenment] succeeds in destroying the West's universal, or intellectually imperialist claims, leaving it to be just another culture." This, he muses, will lead to the destruction of America. Remember the idea of "American exceptionalism" and how we were told it was arrogant to believe such? Bloom was prescient in his firsthand observations. "The lessons students are drawing from their studies," he wrote, "is simply untrue. History and the study of cultures do not teach or prove that values or cultures are relative . . . this premise is unproven and dogmatically asserted for what are largely political reasons."[97]

Students today learn to doubt beliefs even before they believe in anything. No wonder so many young people feel a sense of hopelessness and despair. We can do better than this. Our children deserve better. Any education that removes the importance of faith, values, and the truth about America's religious underpinnings is doing a grave disservice to students. Put simply, Christianity has changed the world for the better. People who are Christians live longer, graduate more, stay out of jail, give more to charity, and contribute more to society than their secular neighbors.

I end this chapter with an admonition about education, given to parents by God through Moses. "Fix these words of mine on your hearts and minds . . . Teach them to your children, talking about them when you sit at home and when you walk along the road, when you lie down and when you get up" (Deuteronomy 11:18, 19). The responsibility for educating the next generation falls squarely on parents. It is, after all, our job. What did God want His people to teach? The moral law. He knew, as did many of the early immigrants to our great country, that education without morality is useless. At best, it is only information. Our children need to know how to responsibly use what they learn. Sadly, higher education does not do this today. Instead, it often undermines the very values parents seek to convey. But we do not have to go along with this educational viewpoint. We can refuse to bow to the god of intellect only and, instead, bow to the God of the universe and ensure our children learn morality in addition to intellectual information.

CHAPTER NINE

All in the Family: Why Alternative Families Fail

*"Fathers have a unique and irreplaceable role in child development.
Fathers are not merely would-be mothers. The two sexes are
different to the core, and each is necessary—culturally as well as
biologically—for the optimal development of a human being."*
−David Popenoe

Professor Robert Oscar Lopez wrote, "I had never given much thought to the possible effect on me of being raised by a lesbian with the help of her lifelong female partner, to the exclusion of my father. I had never considered whether my life was strange because adults who made unusual decisions created, for me, a strange life . . . having been thrown into incomprehensible and bizarre life conditions at an age too young to have any say in the matter."[98]

Lopez had a deep father wound, one that he tried to satisfy, as many young men do, by engaging in homosexual pursuits. He worked in children's television while living a seedy double life as a "gay night crawler." He went into gay prostitution believing older men would embrace him and fill his inexorable emotional void. It did not work; it never does. While Lopez went on to earn his doctoral degree, teach in universities, write books, serve in the military, and speak more than a half-dozen languages, he struggled with his identity. Not until he read the landmark study titled "Social Science on New Family Structures Met with Intolerance" by sociologist Mark Regnerus about the harmful impact of same-sex parenting did he realize his upbringing was far from healthy.

The abstract reads, "Despite claims that 'no differences' exist between children whose parents had a same-sex relationship and children who were raised by their married biological parents, previous research cannot support such an assertion." Using a large, nationally representative dataset, a new study by sociologist Mark Regnerus finds that children whose parents had a same-sex relationship experienced more negative adult outcomes compared with children from intact biological families. The study has sparked a remarkably hostile and unscientific backlash—a backlash presumably motivated by the paper's implications for the same-sex marriage debate. This backlash is regrettable because it undermines the health of public discourse on a subject of enormous significance.

One of the core messages we talk about throughout this book is that for some people—those with specific agendas—facts simply do not matter. They purposely deny facts, science, convention, tradition, and anything else that stands between them and the cultural or moral issues they feel passionate about. It was author Ayn Rand who wrote, "We can ignore reality, but we cannot ignore the consequences of ignoring reality." Here is the truth: children raised by same-sex couples miss out on something and end up struggling to function as adults. They have more trouble functioning at work and school, more difficulty staying in marriages, a greater likelihood of turning to drugs or public assistance to avoid facing life. Why is this issue not considered serious, and why aren't these families placed in an "at risk" group by Social Services? As C.S. Lewis said, "One of the most cowardly things ordinary people do is to shut their eyes to facts."

Hard Truths, Easy Answers

According to Lopez, the one forgotten in all the whirling debate about gay [family] issues is the child. "Children's rights are human rights . . . We have a right to be raised by our mother and father, where possible; and if that isn't possible, to have at the very least a mother and father to love, if a living parent of each sex is available. We have a right to be born free, not bought, sold, or manufactured. Nobody has a 'right' to us. To believe that people can have a 'right' to another person is to believe in slavery."[99]

These alternative families tend to fail at higher rates because they are illegitimate at the very core. In most instances, gay couples adopt children because they cannot have their own. In other words, they take the offspring of normative heterosexual couplings and create a "family" they cannot create because of their own lifestyle choices. In Hollywood, actresses adopt children as if they were pets; gay men and lesbians adopt children—because they can. And we are told matter-of-factly that these unions are just as good for children as traditional families. This is clearly untrue and is unsupported by the research, convention, or outcomes. Two gay men have no idea how to raise a young woman to embrace her femininity. They simply do not have the innate skills to pass along. Nor can two lesbians possibly know what a young boy needs to grow up and embrace masculinity—if they want him to do so (and many do not). You can look at Madonna's adopted son from Malawi, who wears dresses and shared the stage with her at the Pride Variety Show. Actresses Charlize Theron and Angelia Jolie are two other examples of women who decided to adopt Black children, give them everything they could possibly want, and provide photo ops for PEOPLE Magazine and others to show what great parents they are—all without any man involved. Theron recently declared that her seven-year-old daughter is transgender and heartily encourages and endorses it. Seven-years-old! Seriously? Does any child have the slightest idea what they think or think they know at that age? One must wonder, if her daughter said, "Mommy, I think I'm Tinkerbell," if Theron would have affirmed her and bought her a special green dress and wings so she could try to fly. Of course, affirming a child in their misplaced fantasies is not what serious, caring parents do. Helping children grasp the meaning of reality is.

What exactly are the easy answers when it comes to alternative families? First, as we have shown with the Mark Regnerus study, gay parents are inadequate, deficient, harmful, and clearly not up to the task of raising opposite-sex kids no matter how badly they want children. Desire never equals competency. Going back to the experience of Dr. Lopez, he came to understand that his life growing up with two lesbians was far from normal, natural, or nurturing. His long journey was one fraught with deep pain, terrible choices, and eventual freedom when he found faith in Christ. He is now married and has two children. Sadly, good endings are not always the case. As we pointed out earlier, the gay lifestyle is most often anything but gay as it involves higher rates of depression, suicide, STDs, substance abuse, and domestic violence (primarily because a gay lifestyle is most often non-monogamous, which creates tension). But what about other configurations? Perhaps the most notable of alternative families is the one headed by a single parent. How well does this work out for the children?

Family Ties

Sixty-four percent of millennial moms (born between 1982 and 1994) have a child outside of marriage. Nearly half of all millennials think the idea of marriage has become obsolete. As demographics change in the United States, these include one in four children raised in a single-parent home with eighty percent of these being headed by a female. In real numbers, that is 15.6 million children living in a single-mother-headed household.[100]

What does this mean, if anything? Here are a couple obvious observations. First, there is no longer any stigma attached to having children out of wedlock. In some cases, women prefer raising their children without male interference. While this may be rare, it is a growing phenomenon. Second, men who impregnate the women who then become single mothers mostly do so with no repercussions. They simply sow their seed wherever they can; if the woman becomes pregnant, they feel no pressure to hang around. Third, women who become single moms often struggle financially. This equates to a disruption in routines, living spaces, education, and household income. Research is undisputable about the fact that children excel in stable, safe, nurturing environments where their emotional and physical needs are met. Fourth, the financial instability of single-parent households places the burden on taxpayers who are forced to step into the role of providing and protecting where men have abandoned their children. A society that enables and applauds single parenthood does itself a disfavor by silently agreeing to the financial and emotional obligations for the children raised in these homes.

In an era where we hear "my body, my choice," children have little or no choice when parents decide to go it alone. Children inevitably become the victims of these choices raised by single mothers generally struggle with their school achievement, their social and emotional development, their health, and their success in the labor market. These children are at greater risk of parental abuse and neglect (especially from Mom's live-in boyfriends); they are more likely to become teen parents and less likely to graduate from high school or college.[101] Does this sound like a good tradeoff for a healthy society? We know the impacts. The statistics are clear, and the costs are high. Yet, when was the last time you heard a peep about the superiority—and I do not use this word lightly—of traditional marriage in the lives of children? There is no ambiguity here, only clear studies, tragic outcomes, and an unwillingness to address the reasons behind the breakdown of the traditional family.

Researcher David Popenoe thinks he knows the reason. "There are two immediate reasons for the exponential growth of father absence. One is divorce. Fatherlessness caused by non-marital births now virtually equals that caused by divorce, and its effects on children have been shown to be even more deleterious than divorce on children's lives. In most divorce situations, children at least have the advantage of a father's presence for part of their lives. For most children born out of wedlock, the father is out of the picture from the very beginning."[102] He goes on to suggest the greatest single factor in these alternative and single-parent families is the growth of "radical individualism in America, encompassing both men and women." Radical individualism is the idea that nothing else matters except my own happiness. We hear it all the time. "I just need to be true to myself," or "You only live once." Being true to oneself is tantamount to being untrue to someone else. There is always a flipside to our choices in life. When a man asks a woman to marry him, he is saying, "I choose you and un-choose everyone else." It is an exclusive offer. The same is true for a woman who agrees to marriage. She chooses her future husband and forsakes everyone else. The exclusivity of the marriage contract builds safety, harnesses the collective efforts and skills of husband and wife, and creates a secure environment for offspring.

The growing practice of polyamory—a marriage where married couples trade partners to satisfy their sexual needs outside of marriage—is another example of radical individualism that places families and marriages at risk. A whopping one in nine married couples (10.7 percent) have tried a polyamorous relationship, but the results may not have been what they expected. According to a study in the *Frontiers of Psychology*, many of the nearly 3,500 respondents said, "the emotional side of the arrangement was too tricky to navigate." Homosexuals are more likely to engage in multiple sex partners, while heterosexuals couples are less likely.

Asked what people can take away from the study, the lead researcher said, "To keep an open mind. Polyamory won't be for everyone, and that's perfectly OK, but as this study shows, lots of people are thinking about it, and lots of people are practicing it. Rather than judge, it would be wonderful to take the opportunity to learn more about ourselves and our systems; what works and for who and why, some of the benefits, as well as some of the common difficulties, pleasures as well as harms. If we don't talk about it and de-stigmatize it, then we can't learn and understand, and do better by ourselves and our partners."[103] If there is one thing we can say with certainty, it is that judging any behavior—no matter how destructive or self-focused—is not part of the progressives' ideological playbook.

The assumption about non-traditional marriages is that society needs to eliminate any stigma. It is our modern-day view that what people choose to do in the privacy of their own homes or within their own relationships ought to be no one else's business. According to the late Canadian-born American sociologist, socialist, and writer Erving Goffman, "The term stigma is used to refer to an attribute that is deeply discrediting." In terms of social contracts, trust, marriage, and family, stigma can play a positive role. The husband who drives home from work each night, to stop at the bar is exercising his personal rights and autonomy but is neglecting his wife, children, or household obligations. The wife who engages in hours of television, online shopping, or fantasy novels may be placing her marriage at risk and short-changing her children.

When I was a child, it was common practice for people to throw trash out of their cars onto the highways. Similarly, those who smoked often threw out their cigarettes butts. The problem became so bad that lawmakers came up with two solutions. The first was to purposely stigmatize those who threw trash on the highways. The second was to fine those who were caught. "Don't be a litterbug" signs soon appeared along major highways, and fines were imposed to those who failed to heed the warnings. Today, no one wants to be told what they can or cannot do, who they can or cannot sleep with, where they can or cannot go. We live in a culture of destigmatizing bad behavior.

Jesus had no problem calling people out on their bad behaviors. When we remove the boundaries about what constitutes a healthy marriage or family, we weaken society. People who make bad decisions always want to be accepted. Now, however, even the most unhealthy, self-centered lifestyles are part of the mythology that distinctions about behavior do not really matter; only personal happiness does. We are no longer allowed to judge another person's behavior because nothing is bad or good; only what we decide for ourselves matters.

Perfect Families, Imperfect Kids

There is an old saying: "Do you know what a perfect family looks like? No, because it has never happened!" Of course, that is true. But do you know why perfect families do not exist? Because we are imperfect, flawed, selfish, and prone to make mistakes and bad choices. When alternative-family advocates point out that traditional families are flawed, they are absolutely correct. My family was not perfect when I was growing up. I am sure, if you are a mom or dad, you can look back at the mistakes you made along the way and wish you had a do-over. Most of us live with regrets. Most of us wish we had made better choices along our own parenting journey. The Bible is full of stories about dysfunctional families, poor parenting, and sad consequences. You can look at Noah, Moses, Isaac, or David and see how these great men failed to get it right every time. Nevertheless . . .

In study after study, researchers found that despite the imperfections of traditional marriage and family life, it is far superior to *any* other option. Still, Americans continue to believe that cohabitation is an equally viable option to marriage. "Marriage is only a piece of paper" we hear. But is it? As more U.S. adults are delaying marriage—or forgoing it altogether—the share who have at some point lived with an unmarried partner has been on the rise. Amid these changes, most Americans find cohabitation acceptable, even for couples who do not plan to get married, according to a new Pew Research Center survey. The study also found that married adults are more satisfied with their relationship and more trusting of their partners than those who are cohabiting. So while marriage is on the decline, cohabitation is on the rise, despite the fact that higher levels of trust and commitment are essential ingredients to raising children who feel safe and secure.[104]

In his book *Why Marriage Matters*, researcher Glenn T. Stanton looked at the real-life impact of marriage. He found married couples have better physical and mental health. Those in stable marriages showed the lowest lifetime prevalence of alcoholism. He also found the highest suicide rates occur among divorced, widowed, and never married, with the lowest among married. Marital status is also a significant contributor to an individual's state of health and well-being—perhaps the most significant. Married people suffer less from illness and disease and typically enjoy a longer life than those who are not married. The mortality rates are lower too. Divorced men are far more likely to die from disease than their married counterparts. Both single and divorced males are more likely to die from any cause compared with married males. As far as mental health, first-time psychiatric admission rates for males is more than five times as high for non-married men. Paradoxically, feminists have criticized marriage for decades, seeing it as an encumbering and outdated patriarchal institution. Yet women who are married are safer and enjoy better mental health than unmarried women. Researchers have consistently found the highest rates of mental disorder among the divorced and separated, the lowest among married people. Overall, Stanton's findings show married people have lower levels of stress and depression, and greater self-reported happiness.[105]

The research is clear: a two-parent household with a man and a woman, married and committed to one another, is the best possible configuration for children. Nothing else comes close. We know this because of scientific studies that, not surprisingly, hold true across cultures. Why do we keep pretending alternative family structures are equally as healthy for children? The simple answer is some people *need* to believe it. They want to believe their lifestyle choices do not matter. What we now know is they clearly do matter, and they matter most to the kids caught up in this mythology. Researcher Robert Bellah reminds us, "Love becomes a matter of will and action rather than feelings." We have relegated love to feelings, and feelings are ephemeral. For anyone who has been married for an appreciable amount of time, we know feelings can ebb and flow, go through transitions. Bellah adds, "In the evangelical Christian view, love involves placing duty and obligation above the ebb and flow of feelings, and in the end freedom in willing sacrifice of one's own interest to others."[106]

The ideas of duty, obligation, and sacrifice is considered passe, old-school, traditional, backward. The great paradox is this: people who do make these profound commitments and sacrifices are undeniably happier, more fulfilled, and satisfied with their lives and relationships. Great accomplishments in life simply do not happen without sacrifice, and in no place is this more obvious than in the family. As Jesus reminded us, "Greater love has no one than this: to lay down one's life for one's friends" (John 15:13). The notion of radical individualism has spread like cancer in American society to the extent that sacrifice now looks like weakness. A healthy society, a healthy business, a healthy family are not created by individuals who think only of themselves and meeting their own needs. Rather, we create a healthy society by caring about others, working toward a common good, and giving up our insatiable need to feel good all the time.

The Common Good

When we look at alternative relationships and the multiple permutations we are told we must accept lest we be pilloried as bigots and haters, keep in mind that natural law has always favored traditional marriage. Keep in mind also that nonmarital cohabitation favors men more than women. Finally, keep in mind that people who cohabit before marriage lower their chances of later marital success. This may sound counterintuitive in today's world, but those who cohabitate before marriage, if they do eventually choose to marry, have a higher divorce rate than those who do not.

Marriage is a little social institution, and to keep it from ending, couples must make adjustments, solve conflicts, and repair the relationship along the way. These skills are learned, but they also require the kind of commitment many people do not want to make today. They replace that commitment with serial monogamy, untethered relationships, or hookups—none that provide long-term stability for children and none that offer more than transitory pleasure. As David Popenoe observes, "With 50 to 60 percent of parental unions dissolving through divorce, we must be alarmed for children, for families, for society itself."[107]

Where do we go from here? How can we reverse the alternative family trend? We must first recognize that change begins with us—with our relationships, marriage, kids, commitment. We must reverse the feminist disparagement of men and reject the notions of "toxic masculinity" and "patriarchy," terms used to diminish the vital role of fathers in the lives of their families. We must recognize that children need both their mother and father, and that they are better off even if the marriage is imperfect—which, of course, all are. Yes, staying together—in many instances, for the sake of the children—is surprisingly better for children. They are not forced into separate households or exposed to the risks posed by live-in boyfriends or stepparents, which are the number-one reason children are abused in a home.

Through various means, we can all do our part to help young people make the choice for traditional marriage. For instance:

- Encourage our children or grandchildren to embrace time-tested marriage as superior to all other alternatives;
- Be a living example to those around us, mentoring struggling couples, teaching forgiveness and encouraging faithfulness;
- Share our own stories of success and failure;
- Encourage men not to withdraw from their obligations or to accept marginalization from society and home/family life;
- Women can encourage their husbands by showing appreciation and respect, letting them know their role is important in the lives of their children and, though different than the mother's role, every bit as important.

Most men I know are eager to be good dads and loving husbands. There will always be exceptions, but in my experience, men will nearly always step up to the task. I am convinced that most women prefer a masculine man over a weak or passive man. Men in turn need to demonstrate genuine, selfless love to their wives. This begins early on, in the family of origin, where young men learn to treat their moms with kindness.

In summary, we need to recognize that our present culture looks at masculinity as something men are supposed to apologize for. This is nonsense, and good women know it. The media, news, popular culture—all create stereotypes of clueless men and fathers, men who bumble their way through life and marriage, basically useless and out of touch. These false and mocking portrayals of men orchestrate everyday consciousness. Weak men withdraw, check out, abandon their responsibilities, or go into an emotional hole. Strong men shut up and continue their day-to-day responsibilities. As a society, we mock men to our own peril. Is it any wonder we are seeing the rise of weak boys who have no clue what genuine masculinity looks like? The more we push alternative families headed by single-parents or gays and lesbians, the weaker our entire society will become. This weakening of society leads to a form of cultural suicide where our feelings or personal beliefs supplant intuition, science, tradition, and scientific studies about the efficaciousness of traditional marriage and family life.

CHAPTER TEN

Finding Our Way Home

"Then I heard the voice of the Lord saying, 'Whom shall I send? And who will go for us?' And I said, 'Here am I. Send me!'"
–Isaiah 6:8

In the classic movie "The Wizard of Oz," Dorothy longs for a place that is normal, a place like home. "Someplace where there isn't any trouble," she says. "Do you suppose there is such a place, Toto? There must be." We each yearn for continuity and predictability. A safe place. If you have done a lot of traveling, you know what it is like to come home. For most of us, we find comfort going back to what we know—to our own bed, our familiar surroundings. The environment we find ourselves in today, however, is anything but normal, comfortable, or even predictable. It is as if our world has been hijacked by lunatics, yet the lunatics do not realize how unstable they are.

Nor do they realize the repercussions of their irrational worldviews, behaviors—or the consequences. Unfortunately, their ideas impact the rest of us. It reminds me of a deranged passenger who tries to open the door of an airliner. Other passengers may sit back and say to themselves, "It's not my problem; someone else can intervene." The problem with this attitude is that if no one steps in to stop the madman, everyone on the flight will die once the cabin is depressurized. There are times in life when we are forced to act, not because we want to but because we must. We live in such a time.

Grumbling vs. Gratitude

It was John Adams who said, "I am well aware of the toil and blood and treasure that it will cost to maintain this Declaration and support and defend these States. Yet through all the gloom I can see rays of ravishing light and glory. I can see that the end is worth more than all the means." In their book *The Light and the Glory: Did God have a plan for America?*, Peter Marshall and David Manuel painstakingly examined the history of America, our early beginnings, and the incredible Divine providence that has led us to become the light to the world. Our light, I am sad to say, is barely a flicker today. The authors wrote, "It is the most dangerous kind of corporate self-delusion to think that a President, regardless of how much he heeds God, can reverse the bent of the national will, once it is set in a certain direction."[108]

The history of the Jewish people may soon become the history of the American republic. God called forth this tribe of people who were enslaved in Egypt working the limestone, basalt, and mud-brick pits. He called them to Himself to represent

His purposes to the rest of the world. Yes, chosen and rescued by God. Yet, their exodus from Egypt was far from smooth. Freedom rarely is. The people complained, rebelled, disobeyed, and eventually wanted to go back to the very place where they were in bondage. Why? Because it represented the known. The Promised Land? What was that? They had no idea. They preferred the familiar bondage and slavery of Egypt to unfamiliar freedom in Canaan. Though God had delivered them from the slavery of Egypt, they had not yet experienced all that God had in store for them. In reality, they could not even imagine how good it could be.

In America today, we *have* experienced the goodness of God. We have seen His hand at work from the very beginning—a history of self-discovery that has led to the freedoms we enjoy today. And yet, like many of the Jews in the desert, we complain about what we do not have; for the Hebrews, it was water or the right kind of food. They did not yet know how to handle their newfound freedom. They knew what they were free from, but they did not know what to do with that freedom. They had no appreciation for it. Look at how these newly freed slaves handled their freedom: *They raised their voices and wept aloud. All the Israelites grumbled* (see Numbers 14:1-2).

The people went on to say, "If only we had died in Egypt! Or in this wilderness! Why is the Lord bringing us to this land only to let us fall by the sword? Our wives and children will be taken as plunder. Wouldn't it be better for us to go back to Egypt?" (verses 2-3). Like so many of us, they assumed the worst. In so doing, it became their destiny. An entire generation was not allowed to enter the freedom God had for them.

God gave them food and water in the desert. He gave them a cloud by day and a pillar of fire by night. He opened the Red Sea so they could pass through. He gave them rules to live by so things would go well for them. And yet, when He took them to the border of the Promised Land, they complained. After all the miracles, they still did not believe God would come through for them. Human nature? I think it is more than that; it is ingratitude.

Perhaps that is where we are in America today. We lack trust in God—and gratitude for all He has done for us. We lack trust in His ability to rescue us. We do not trust He has our best interests in mind. Perhaps we give lip service to Him, but do we really believe He will come through for us in such a time as this? God delights in our trust, even when we do not have a clear path ahead—*especially* if we do not have a clear path. And as we learn from the history of the Jewish nation, God has limits and will tolerate ingratitude and distrust only so long before acting. This was true of the Great Flood in Noah's time, the Tower of Babel, and sending the Jewish people into exile. Is modern America better or worse than pre-flood times? What about Sodom and Gomorrah? Are we better or worse? How long will God's patience last? We look on in stunned disbelief at the things going on around us, thinking we will wake up from a bad dream and everything will go back to normal. I am no doomsday prophet. To the contrary, I still believe we live in the greatest nation on earth, and this greatness did not happen by accident. It was intentional. Our founders had seen what happens when men rule with impunity. As a result, they created checks and balances into our government—the executive, legislative, and judicial branches. The latter is currently under increasing attack by people who do not like decisions coming out of the highest court.

What Matters Most

If you grew up around the ocean, you know what a riptide is. The odd thing about a riptide is the person caught in it rarely recognizes his problem until it is too late. It can be subtle. It can be sudden. It can be deadly. Metaphorically, we are swimming in waters where riptides are pulling us out from shore and into the wide-open ocean. We are willingly swimming in these hazardous waters, and many of us do not know it. Lifeguards save the lives of unwitting swimmers every year. In a sense, you and I are lifeguards, trying to get the attention of imperiled swimmers and encouraging them to return to shore, to a safe haven. We know some swimmers will say, "I know what's best for me," or "Everything is fine; don't overreact." They may realize the seriousness of their plight only after it is too late. Again, that is where we find ourselves in today's chaotic moral environment. If your child is drowning, what do you do? You act—and act fast. I believe that is where we are as a country right now. Many may think they can wade part way into the ocean because it is still safe. This can be a fatal mistake as rogue waves and fast currents can easily pull us into the ocean.

How do we save someone who deliberately places themselves or others in the way of danger? What do we do with the guy who is trying to pry open the airliner's exit door or force open the cockpit door during flight? Doing nothing places all of us at risk. Waiting for others to step in only wastes precious time and increases the chance of catastrophe. If we haven't figured it out by now, what I am saying is that ALL of us must keep that guy from opening the door in flight. We cannot wait; we must act. We must act to keep people out of the riptides of life, even those who do not recognize the danger they are in or the danger they place others in. Remember the story of Cain and Abel? After Cain murdered his brother, Abel, God asked, "Where is your brother Abel?" Cain replied, "I don't know. Am I my brother's keeper?" (Genesis 4:8-9). Not only did Cain lie to God, but his answer completely missed the point: of course, we are our brother's keeper. This is certainly true today.

I often wonder why God is so patient with us. Why does He put up with smart-aleck comments or questions like Cain threw at Him? The Bible—from front to back—is God's way of revealing Himself to us, working to draw us to Himself, and helping us understand how to live our lives in ways that honor His plans and purposes for us. He also wants us to love our neighbors as ourselves, which is one of the Ten Commandments. This begs a vital question: what is our purpose in life? It is simply to honor God with whatever skills and gifts He has implanted within us. As theologian Os Guinness says, "Answering the call of our Creator is therefore the highest purpose on the journey." He goes on to ask, "What is meant by 'calling'? Simply that God calls us to Himself so decisively that everything we are, everything we do, and everything we have is invested with special devotion and dynamism lived out as a response to His summons and service."[109] In answer to the question about what matters most, surely the first and most direct answer is our relationship with our Creator. Nothing else comes close. It is from this relationship and understanding of our obligations as "our brother's keeper" that we engage in right action, which is always preceded by right thinking. Never forget that we have the moral, practical, and scientific high ground in this culture war we have been forced to fight.

What Can I Do?

First, remember that people of faith comprise some of the greatest thinkers in history. Contrary to what the so-called progressives want you to believe, great men and women of faith have done extraordinary things throughout the ages. A short list includes Augustine, Dante, Gutenberg, Pascal, Rembrandt, da Vinci, Copernicus, Galileo, Bacon, Newton, Bach, Handel, Mozart, Wilberforce, Dostoevsky, Faraday, Lord Kelvin, Marconi, and George Washington Carver. In chemistry, earth sciences, physics and astronomy, mathematics, medicine—Christians have been seminal leaders and inventors. As many of our public schools are taken captive by radicals who seek to destroy Christian history and relegate it to the ash heap of progressivism, remember those God used to make us a great nation.

Second, we read in the Book of Exodus that Moses complained to God that he was not eloquent and could not speak well, so therefore he could not do the task God had called him to do. In response, God asked Moses an interesting question: "Who gave human beings their mouths?" God had called Moses into service, but Moses said, "Please send someone else to do it" (Exodus 4:11-13). That angered the Lord. In fact, verse 14 says "… the LORD's anger burned against Moses." You and I, like Moses, have a mouth. We have influence. Maybe we do not lead a huge church, host a podcast, or speak to a large audience, but we do have a mouth. We can speak. Will there be a cost? Undoubtedly. Maybe we will lose a friend or two. Maybe people will become angry or offended. That should not stop us. We need to get past the idea that we must appease people who hate what we stand for. If we are people pleasers, we need to learn to speak the truth in love, and let God deal with the resulting feelings or repercussions. Those who want to dismantle our nation have so far faced little resistance. They need to know how we feel and what we think. The facts speak from themselves—in marriage and family, in the LGBTQ+, on racial issues, abortion, education, drugs, homelessness, borders—we must speak up, speak out, and not apologize for doing so. Truth is not always something people want to hear or embrace, but it still needs to be heard. As the prophet Jeremiah wrote, "Their ears are closed so they cannot hear. The word of the LORD is offensive to them; they find no pleasure in it" (Jeremiah 6:10).

Third, we need to learn to trust the truth. Many devout Jewish men wear a small leather box on their forehead or left arm during their daily prayers. These boxes, called phylacteries, contain Bible texts that serve as reminders of God's Word and His immutable laws. God gave us those moral laws for a reason. His laws are not suggestions or subjective ideas based on feelings or random ideas, but rather His inerrant and unchanging word. I encourage you to apply the issues we have covered in the previous chapters to objective moral laws. For example, property rights exist to protect homeowners, much like boundaries or borders exist to protect a country and its citizens. If people are permitted to come into our home or onto our property uninvited, we are left with no way to protect our family or our possessions. Speaking of property rights, as businesses leave blue (progressive) states and cities to relocate in red (conservative) states and cities, most are doing so because they cannot operate at a profit when the homeless or drug addicts are allowed to harass their employees, shoot up outside their stores, or steal their merchandise.

Fourth, we need to attend public meetings, ask questions, take notes. In recent years, we have seen parents show up at schoolboard meetings and ask members questions about curriculum, book choices, and DEI programs. Many progressive leaders do not like questions. They want to be left alone or decide policy in closed meetings without input or interference. If we do not show up, ask questions, take notes, and hold leaders accountable in city government, county commissions, schoolboards, or library districts, we will see these institutions taken over by progressive elitists who believe parents are the enemy, and dissent is disruptive.

Fifth, maybe Moses could not speak that well, but he sure could write! We know he wrote the first five books of the Bible and at least 125,000 words. We can do the same. We can write letters to the editor in our local papers. And we need to keep them short and on point. Believe it or not, the letters-to-the-editor sections are read by 37 percent of newspaper readers. If no one writes opposing opinion pieces, others will believe no one cares. We can express ourselves to retailers about their support for drag shows, DEI, or other core issues covered in this book. When a retailer asks for a review, we can include comments about the causes they support, good or bad. We know some retailers are committed to immoral causes—Google, Wells Fargo, Starbucks, North Face, Target, Budweiser, Ben & Jerrys, Bank of America, Levis, Gillette, PayPal, Nike, Disney, and most airlines. Tell retailers their policies are offensive, then tell them why. Boycott those who are disinterested in hearing your voice.

Sixth, learn to discern. When a teller touches a $100 bill, in most instances she can tell immediately if it is counterfeit. How can she do this? It comes from handling money all day long. She has become so accustomed to what is authentic that when she feels the counterfeit, she knows it is a fake. We need to develop that sort of discernment so we can know and embrace truth, which will enable us to know when we are being duped. Where does truth emanate? From my perspective and experience, the Bible serves as the ultimate guide to moral decision-making. For radical secularists, they may reject the Bible as a source of truth. But natural law is an effective tool for discussing moral truth. Edmund Burke was essentially a Christian statesman who believed God's laws were innate, or as the Apostle Paul said, the law was written on all men's hearts, even those who do not follow God (see Romans 2:15). Burke wrote, "Moral prudence and historical continuity, rather than the raw, untried, arbitrary, and isolated speculations of any man's private reason, should determine the extent and manner of social reform."[110] What Burke was saying is that one's personal experience or feelings is inadequate for formulating policies.

Seventh, we must learn to trust our intuition. In the dark movie *The Girl with the Dragon Tattoo*, Martin Vanger, played by actor Stellan Skarsgard, asks Daniel Craig a telling question before he proceeds to torture him in a secret chamber beneath his home. "Let me ask you something. Why don't people trust their instincts? They sense something is wrong; someone is walking too close behind them . . . You knew something was wrong, but you came back into the house. Did I force you? Did I drag you in? No. All I had to do was offer you a drink. It's hard to believe that the fear of offending can be stronger than the fear of pain." The scene is a powerful reminder that we tend to ignore our intuition. If we feel uncomfortable about a teacher, a place, a comment—question it. We can trust ourself; God has given us a conscience for a reason.

Eighth, teach our children well. We can teach them to think clearly, to act wisely, to communicate effectively. This is not the time for free-range parenting. Listen to what the Apostle Paul wrote: "The wrath of God is being revealed from heaven against all the godlessness and wickedness of people, who suppress the truth by their wickedness, since what may be known about God is plain to them . . . people are without excuse" (Romans 1:18-20). Paul goes on to say there are consequences for deliberately ignoring God's design. ". . . the men also abandoned natural relations with women and were inflamed with lust for one another. Men committed shameful acts with other men, and received in themselves the due penalty for their error" (verses 26-27). We must teach our children there are natural consequences to poor choices. We also need to encourage them to make the right choices and let them see the good consequences that come from right actions.

Ninth—and it pains me to say this—many churches are more interested in keeping people happy than in keeping them accountable. These compromised churches teach what people want to hear, what makes listeners feel good. They do not want to offend anybody. They are quick to remind us that "God is love." Yes, He is, but He also has expectations. As parents, we love our children, but we still have expectations. We discipline them when they need it—because we love them. These churches teach a partial gospel by leaving out the hard parts. For example, while the Bible is clear about homosexuality, some churches embrace the idea of "gay Christianity" as if this is the loving thing to do. Where does this end? Do we also embrace "pedophile Christians" because to do otherwise would be unloving? We must not apologize for moral truth. We must not compromise, adjust, redefine, re-interpret, justify, or rationalize it. Remember, the owner's manual is written by the manufacturer for a reason.

Finally, do not underestimate the battle we are in. The drag queens at a pride march in New York are not kidding when they chant, "We're here, we're queer, we're coming for your children." It was the Apostle Paul who wrote, "For our struggle is not against flesh and blood, but against the rulers, against the authorities, against the powers of this dark world and against the spiritual forces of evil in the heavenly realms" (Ephesians 6:12). This should be a sober reminder that what we are dealing with in our country is not just red and blue, conservative and liberal—it is a spiritual battle between good and evil, right and wrong. Our kids and grandkids, our marriage, our school, community, leaders—all are in the crosshairs. Perhaps you have heard the saying "God loves you and has a wonderful plan for your life." That is a feel-good truth that comes with a corollary few people talk about: "The enemy hates you and has a plan to destroy your life." Satan is our enemy, and he comes to rob, kill, and destroy (see John 10:10). We must be on our guard, be vigilant, be aware. We must not panic, retreat, or be afraid. If God is for us, then no man, no ideas, no lies will prevail (see Romans 8:28). We can go forth in the strength of truth—the strength of Almighty God.

ABOUT THE AUTHORS

Michael A. Letts is the Founder, President, and CEO of In-Vest USA, a national grassroots non-profit organization that is helping hundreds of communities provide thousands of bullet-proof vests for their police forces through educational, public relations, sponsorship, and fundraising programs.

As of January 2021, more than 6,500 concealable and active shooter vests have been distributed to police officers throughout the United States, and globally as the result of his leadership and passion. The organization's efforts have helped police officers from areas devastated by Hurricane Katrina to nations such as Nicaragua and Mexico. In addition to his national efforts, Letts is actively involved in political and community service in South Carolina. He is the Governor's Appointee on the S.C. Legislative Infrastructure Study Committee, a member of the South Carolina Policy Council, and SLED Chaplain with the South Carolina Law Enforcement Division and the Columbia Police Department.

As a Councilman on the Central Midlands Council of Governments, he served on the executive, finance, transportation, and environmental-planning committees. He holds numerous leadership positions in the Chamber of Commerce, Boy Scouts of America, and Kiwanis. His involvement has earned him a Congressional Gold Medal Award for Community Service and the SC Order of the Palmetto, South Carolina's highest civilian honor for extraordinary lifetime achievement and service to the state and nation. His efforts have been recognized globally with the bestowing of the title **His Excellency Count, Sir Michael A. von Letts, Chevalier, Knight of Honor of the Imperial Teutonic Order,** by the Republic of Germany.

Letts has a passion for the educational needs of our children, and the need to ensure that our next generation becomes the first responders we have a shortage of today. This is evidenced by his founding of The First Responder Academy Public Charter High School, and Hope Academy (Infant—K-5). He has also launched the "Pennies for Police" initiative through In-Vest USA, aimed at allowing our children to support and interface with their school resource officer by helping to provide that officer with a bulletproof vest. This program is a vital part of his efforts to "Save a Kid—Save a Cop". He initiated the acclaimed "Bless the Vest" program that works with Houses of Worship partnering the congregations with their local first responders to provide physical, emotional, and spiritual support.

A successful businessman, Letts is the Founder and President of Salty Fin Realty and Holdings and various other business ventures, as well as a member of the First Palmer Family Trust, Letts is also an ordained minister and was Executive Pastor/Music Minister of the Eastside Baptist Church. He earned his B.S. in Business Administration from Liberty University in 1985. He resides in Columbia, S.C., with his wife and partner, Karen. For more information, go to: www.michaelletts.us

Don S. Otis has thirty years of experience managing corporate media, author-publicity campaigns, and overseeing creative-media writing and immediate-response releases through his company Veritas Communications. He has written four traditionally published books, and his writing has appeared in such publications as *Focus on the Family, Charisma, ParentLife, Living with Teenagers, Light & Life,* and *Christian Single.*

Otis lived and worked in the Middle East where he managed the clandestine Voice of Hope Radio Network. Later, he helped start what became known as Middle East Television. He served as manager to a multi-cultural and ethnically diverse staff and as liaison between the Israeli Defense Forces (IDF), the United Nations (UNIFIL), and the South Lebanese militia.

ENDNOTES

1   Dietrich Bonhoeffer, *The Cost of Discipleship* (New York: McMillian Publishing, 1949) p. 239.

2   https://www.axios.com/local/philadelphia/2022/09/20/philadelphia-homicide-violent-crime

3   https://6abc.com/philadelphia-news-philly-budget-cuts

4   https://www.foxnews.com/politics/austin-texas-defunded-its-police-department-now-voters-will-decide-if-city-needs-more-officers

5   yahoo.com/news/Washington-property-owner-say-squatters

6   Os Guinness, *Long Journey Home* , (Colorado Springs, Waterbrook Press, 2001), p. 29, 36.

7   Robert H. Bellah, *The Good Society* (New York: Vintage Books, 1991), p. 3-4.

8   Judith Wallerstein, *Second Chances* (New York: Tricknor & Fields, 1989), p. xxi.

9   Ibid, p. 234.

10 Teri Reisser with Paul Reiser M.D., *A Solitary Sorrow* (Wheaton, IL: Shaw Publishers, 1989) pp 30-31.

11 https://www.huffpost.com/entry/debbie-squires-education-official-says-teachers-know-better-than-parents_n_1264025

12 Thomas Jefferson's "Commonplace Book," 1774-1776,

quoting from *On Crimes and Punishment* by criminologist Cesare Beccaria, 1764.

13 Greg Wehner of FoxNews.com said on February 23, 2023, "St. Louis suspect seen calmly loading gun, shooting homeless man execution-style in broad daylight."

14 John Binder, www.breitbart.com/politics/2023/02/20/study-70-percent-suspects-freed-from-jail-without-bail-re-arrested

15 https://www.heritage.org/firearms/report/fact-sheet-gun-violence

16 https://joebiden.com/gunsafety/#

17 David Popenoe, *Life Without Father* (New York: The Free Press, 1996), p. 3.

18 childtrends.org

19 Popenoe, *Father.*

20 Kurt W. Back, *Social Psychology* (New York: John Wiley & Sons, 1977), p. 396.

21 https://www.yesmagazine.org/opinion/2022/06/13/end-mass-shootings-violent-culture

22 https://nypost.com/2022/02/11/accused-santa-fe-school-shooter-dimitrios-pagourtzis-still-not-mentally-fit-for-trial/

23 M. Scott Peck, *People of the Lie* (New York, Touchstone, 1983), p. 105.

24 Ibid, p. 43.

25 C.S. Lewis, *Screwtape Letters* (New York, MacMillian, 1960), p. vii.

26 Hannah Grossman, "Arizona school board member says district should reject hiring teachers with Christian values: 'Not . . . safe,'" FoxNews.com, 3 March, 2023.

27 Sheetal Malhotra, "Impact of Sexual Revolution: Consequences of Risky behaviors," Journal of American Physicians

and Surgeons, Volume 13 Number 3, Fall 2008 -- https://www.jpands.org/vol13no3/malhotra.pdf

28 Scott Yenor, "A Postmortem on the Sexual Revolution: What Deregulation of Pornography Has Wrought," The Heritage Foundation, 19 May 2020 -- https://www.heritage.org/marriage-and-family/report/postmortem-the-sexual-revolution-what-deregulation-pornography

29 Brian Clowes, PhD, "Is Homosexual behavior really as Healthy as Heterosexual?" Human Life International, 9 June 2020 -- https://www.hli.org/resources/homosexuality-is-not-a-healthy-lifestyle

30 Rikki Schlott, "Trans battle in sports is erasure of what a woman is," ex-Kentucky swimmer Riley Gaines says," *New York Post*, 2 March 2023. https://nypost.com/2023/03/02/riley-gaines-trans-athletes-competing-with-women-not-progressive/

31 Alexander Hall, "Twitter laughs, groans as Jill Biden gives biological male Women of Courage award: 'Up your game, ladies,' FoxNews.com, 8 March 2023.

32 Os Guinness, *Unriddling Our Times* (Grand Rapids, Michigan: Baker Books, 1999). P. 67.

33 Allan Bloom, *The Closing of the American Mind* (New York: Touchstone, 1987), p. 28.

34 Carrie Sheffield, "Behind teen girls' sky-high depression: Forced sex, social media," New York Post, 24 February 2023.

35 Robert Bork, *Slouching Toward Gomorrah: Modern Liberalism and American Decline,* (New York: HarperCollins, 1996), p. 4.

36 Wallerstein, *Chances*, p. xv.

37 Glenn T. Stanton, *Why Marriage Matters* (Colorado Springs:

Pinion, 1997), pp 74-90.

38 www.msn.com/en-us/news/other/planned-parent-hood-alumni-launch-ai-chatbot-encouraging-abortion

39 Francis Shaeffer, *The Great Evangelical Disaster* (Westchester, IL: Crossway, 1984) pp. 22-23.

40 William L. Shirer, *The Rise and Fall of the Third Reich* (New York: Simon and Schuster, 1960), p. 656.

41 C. Everett Koop, M.D. Francis Schaeffer, *Whatever Happened to the Human Race* (Westchester, IL: Crossway, 1987), p. 81.

42 TOP 25 QUOTES BY MOTHER TERESA (of 878) | A-Z Quotes (azquotes.com)

43 *A Solitary Sorrow* (Wheaton, Illinois: Shaw Publishers, 1999), P. 97, 25.

44 https://anglicansforlife.org/2020/06/17/aborted-black-babies/

45 *War in the Wilderness* (Nashville, Tennessee, Randall House, 2023), p. 41.

46 Joseph Goebbels Quotes About Lying | A-Z Quotes (azquotes.com)

47 https://www.goodreads.com/author/quotes/2782.Viktor_E_Frankl

48 *Long Journey Home* (Colorado Springs, Colorado, Waterbrook Press, 2001) p. 201.

49 https://www.breitbart.com/crime/2023/03/28/trans-activists-pushed-aggressive-rhetoric-before-shooting-at-christian-school/

50 Julia Romero, "Mothers of teens accused of running down former California police chief speak out," 21 September, 2023—www.yahoo.com/news/mothers-teens-accused-running-down-200647618.

51 Charles Colson, *Kingdoms in Conflict* (Grand Rapids, Michigan, 1987) p. 231.

52 Andrea Vacchiano, "San Francisco supervisor Hillary Ronen begs for more police after voting to defund in 2020," <u>Fox News</u>, 19 March, 2023.

53 https://www.kxan.com/investigations/homicides-on-the-rise-how-austin-compares-to-other-big-cities

54 https://www.foxnews.com/us/police-defunded-cities-murders-crime-budget/

55 https://nypost.com/2019/12/16/barr-rising-disrespect-for-cops-not-only-wrong-it-puts-us-in-danger

56 Arkansas cop 'ambushed, executed' in fatal shooting near station (nypost.com)

57 Robert Bellah, *Habits of the Heart* (New York, Harper & Row, 1985) p. 65.

58 https://abcnews.go.com/US/crimes-rise-battles-rage-police-funding/story

59 https://www.politifact.com/article/2007/sep/01/how-much-credit-giuliani-due-fighting-crime/

60 https://www.foxnews.com/us/rodney-king-trial-a-look-back-at-the-racially-charged-high-profile-case

61 https://www.heritage.org/povery-and-inequality/report/the-war-poverty-after-50-years

62 Ibid.

63 www.breitbart.com/politics/2023/03/21/white-fragility-author-robin-diangelo-says-people-color-need-get-away-white-people/

64 Hannah Grossman, Pentagon disbands DEI unit after chief accused of 'racism' against whites . injects agenda deeper into agency," <u>Fox News</u>, 31 March 2023.

65 Jeffery Clark, "Oklahoma Democrat state rep appears to condone worship of woke priorities: 'DEI is 'God.'" <u>Fox News</u>, 8 March 2023.

66 *Critical Dilemma: The Rise of Critical Theories and Social Justice Ideology—Implications for the Church and Society* (Eugene: Harvest House Publishers, 2023).

67 Bork, *Slouching*, p. 245.

68 Ibid., pp. 240-241.

69 Dr. Jordan Peterson, *12 Rules for Life: An Antidote to Chaos* (Toronto: Random House, 2018), p. 281.

70 https://www.pewresearch.org/fact-tank/2021/11/08/whats-behind-the-growing-gap-between-men-and-women-in-college-completion/

71 Bloom, *Closing*, p. 96).

72 Martin Luther King, Jr., "Loving Your Enemies," Dexter Avenue Baptist Church, December 17, 1957.

73 www.washingtonexaminer.com/report-nearly-all-998-of-illegal-drugs-shipped-to-us-from-mexico

74 www.cbsnews.com/news/fentanyl-seizures-rise-u-s-mexico-border-heres-why/

75 Peterson, *12 Rules*, p. 87.

76 Ibid., p. xiv.

77 Judith Wallerstein, *Second Chances* (New York: Tecknor & Fields, 1989), pp. 24-25.

78 Ibid., p. 25.

79 Popenoe, *Father*, pp. 2-3.

80 Robert Bly, *Iron John* (Cambridge, Massachusetts, Da Capo Press 2004) p. 15.

81 Ibid., p. 61.

82 Jeffery Clark, "Gen Z hardest generation to work with," <u>Fox News</u>, 26 April 2023.

83 Dr. Gregory Jantz and Michael Gurian, *Raising Boys By Design* (Colorado Springs, CO WaterBrook Press, 2013), p. 56.

84 William Bennett, *The Moral Compass* (New York: Simon & Schuster, 1995). pp. 483-484.

85 Kathleen Moore, "UAlbany students shout down conservative speaker," Times Union, 6 April 2023.

86 Bloom, *American Mind*, p. 61.

87 https://nypost.com/2022/04/24/randi-weingartens-latest-anti-parent-rantings-are-extreme

88 https://www.businessinsider.com/us-ranks-27th-for-health-care-and-education-2018

89 https://www.insider.com/how-much-countries-around-the-world-spend-on-education-2019-8

90 "Why Randi Weingarten Supports Harvard's Discrimination," Allysia Finley, Wall Street Journal, 30 October 2022.

91 https://news.yahoo.com/asian-american-student-1590-sat-71857237.html?fr=sycsrp_catchall

92 https://nypost.com/2022/11/23/mike-pompeo-slams-teachers-union-head-randi-weingarten-as-dangerous/

93 Charles Creitz, "Zionist and conservative students are terrified to express their views on campus" FOX News, 7 May 2023.

94 Ibid.

95 Betsy McCaughey, "What teachers unions do is legalized thuggery: Here's what parents can do," FOX News.com, 27 April 2023.

96 https://www.cbsnews.com/atlanta/news/dei-programs-in-universities-are-being-cut-across-the-country-what-does-this-mean-for-higher-education/

97 Bloom, *American Mind*, p. 39.

98 Robert Oscar Lopez, *Jephthah's Daughters: Innocent casualties in the war for family "equality"* (Los Angeles: International Children's Rights Institute, 2015), pp 23, 26.

99 Ibid.

100 https://www.wealthysinglemommy.com/single-mom-statistics

101 https://www.brookings.edu/opinions/are-children-raised-with-absent-fathers-worse-off

102 Popenoe, *Father*, p. 192.

103 https://www.newsweek.com/polyamorous-relationship-one-nine-americans-study-1594618

104 https://www.pewresearch.org/social-trends/2019/11/06/marriage-and-cohabitation-in-the-u-s/

105 Glenn T, Stanton, *Why Marriage Matters: Reasons to Believe in Marriage in Postmodern Society* (Colorado Springs: Pinon Press, 1997), pp 71-90.

106 Robert Bellah, *Habits of the Heart: individualism and Commitment in American Life* (New York: Harper & Row, 1985), pp 95-96.

107 Popenoe, *Father*, p. 222.

108 Peter Marshall and David Manuel, *The Light and the Glory: Did God have a plan for America?* (Grand Rapids: Fleming H. Revell, 1977) p. 356.

109 Guinness, *Unriddling*, pp.212-213.

110 Peter J. Stanlis, *Edmund Burke and the Natural Law* (Lafayette: Huntington House, 1986), p. 165.

A free ebook edition is available with the purchase of this book.

To claim your free ebook edition:

1. Visit MorganJamesBOGO.com
2. Sign your name CLEARLY in the space
3. Complete the form and submit a photo of the entire copyright page
4. You or your friend can download the ebook to your preferred device

Morgan James BOGO™

A **FREE** ebook edition is available for you or a friend with the purchase of this print book.

CLEARLY SIGN YOUR NAME ABOVE

Instructions to claim your free ebook edition:
1. Visit MorganJamesBOGO.com
2. Sign your name CLEARLY in the space above
3. Complete the form and submit a photo of this entire page
4. You or your friend can download the ebook to your preferred device

Print & Digital Together Forever.

Snap a photo

Free ebook

Read anywhere

Printed in the USA
CPSIA information can be obtained
at www.ICGtesting.com
LVHW090035270924
792159LV00004B/14